The Story of God and His People

Hope of the World

Rachelle Wiersma

CHRISTIAN SCHOOLS INTERNATIONAL
3350 East Paris Ave. SE
Grand Rapids, Michigan 49512-3054

Printed in the United States of America

10 9 8 7 6 5 4 3 2

ISBN 0-87463-976-X

The development of this book was made possible with grants from Christian Schools International Foundation and Canadian Christian Education Foundation, Inc.

Photographs: Neal and Joel Bierling, Phoenix Data Systems: 8, 11, 19, 21, 23, 29, 39, 48, 50, 55, 66, 68, 76, 78, 85, 94, 96, 101, 104, 110, 113, 115, 121, 123, 129, 131, 143, 144, 147, 156, 160, 161, 171; JHM: 25, 27, 37, 63, 73, 74, 138; Superstock: 40, 52, 59, 61, 70, 82, 88, 92, 126, 164, 166, 169, 173, 175.

Contents

Setting the Stage for Jesus' Ministry

1 The Western Political World During the Intertestamentary Period

Daniel 2

The time between the Old and the New Testaments is sometimes referred to as the silent years. Some people might think that not much was taking place in the world during these 400 years, but actually a great deal was happening in the Western world during that time. These events would prepare the world for the coming of Christ. The Persians, whose ruler allowed the Jews to return to Jerusalem and to rebuild the temple and the walls, eventually gave way to the Greeks.

Alexander the Great led the Greeks. Within 10 years of beginning his conquests, he had conquered Persia and Egypt and even extended the boundaries of his empire into India. Alexander encouraged the spread of the Greek language and culture. Because the Jews were dispersed throughout the Greek empire, the Hebrew Old Testament was translated into Greek in Alexandria, Egypt. This Greek Old Testament came to be known as the Septuagint. The New Testament would later be written in Greek, which was then the universal language of the Western world.

Statue of Zeus, 470 B.C.

Alexander's unexpected death led to the division of the Greek empire among Alexander's generals. For the Jews living in Palestine this division was initially positive. Alexander's general Ptolemy was given control over the southern section of the Middle

Timeline 445 B.C.–A.D. 70

445 B.C.	Nehemiah rebuilds Jerusalem's walls
334 B.C.	Alexander begins Persian campaigns
333 B.C.	Alexander defeats Darius II of Persia
323 B.C.	Alexander dies at Babylon
250 B.C.	Hebrew Scriptures are translated into Greek
167 B.C.	Zeus is worshiped in the temple at Jerusalem
141 B.C.	Jews liberate Jerusalem
63 B.C.	Pompey captures Jerusalem
47 B.C.	Antipater becomes ruler of Judea
44 B.C.	Julius Caesar is assassinated
37 B.C.	Herod the Great becomes king of Judea until 4 B.C.
31 B.C.	Augustus becomes emperor of Rome
3 B.C.	Approximate date of Jesus' birth at Bethlehem
A.D. 30	Approximate date of Jesus' crucifixion
A.D. 45	Paul begins missionary journeys
A.D. 54	Nero becomes emperor of Rome
A.D. 66	Jewish revolt
A.D. 70	Titus destroys Jerusalem

East, including Egypt. The Ptolemaic kings allowed the Jews to live in relative peace and to worship God as they desired in the Jerusalem temple.

Later Palestine was captured by the Seleucid kings, whose capital was Damascus in Syria. These northern kings were descended from Alexander's general Seleucus. When these Greeks conquered Judea, many upper-class Jews were attracted to the Greek culture they brought with them. Those Jews who remained true to God and their Jewish culture were outraged when the Seleucids forced the worship of Greek gods on them. The final insult for these faithful Jews came when sacrifices to Zeus were made in the Jerusalem temple.

These sacrifices to Zeus resulted in a Jewish revolt (166 B.C.). The Maccabees, a family of priests, led this revolt. Under the leadership of Judas Macabeus, Palestine was freed from foreign rule for the first time in 450 years. Judas rededicated the temple in Jerusalem and guided the people in worshiping God. As long as

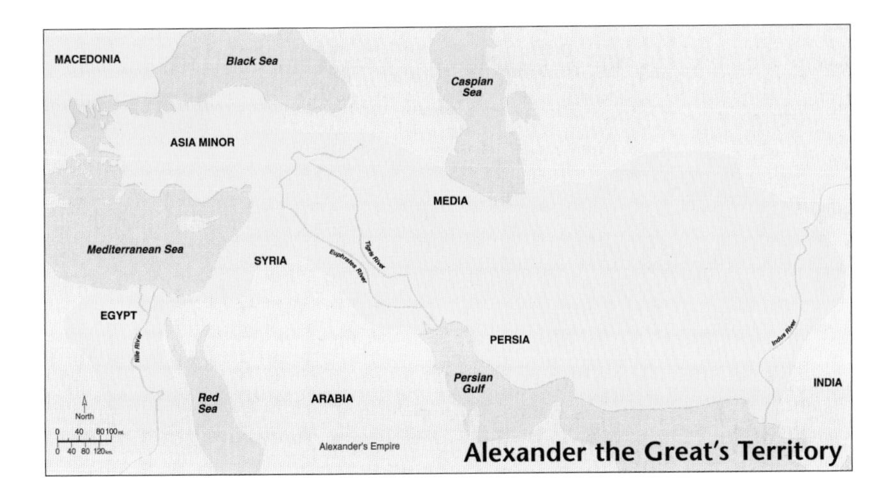

Alexander the Great's Territory

the Maccabees served as good rulers and priests, their rule was effective. (Another name for the Maccabeans is the Hasmoneans.)

A quarrel in the Maccabean family led them to seek advice from Rome, the new world power. Rather than settle the dispute, the Romans made Palestine a Roman province in 63 B.C. Leadership of the Roman Empire was not firmly established until 31 B.C., when Augustus became the first Roman emperor. Unlike his predecessors, Augustus did not seek to expand the borders of the Roman Empire. Instead, he worked to peacefully maintain the borders that already existed. This period of peace became known as the *Pax Romana.*

God chose this time in world history to send his Son, Jesus. The Roman Empire had been at peace for about 25 years at the time of Jesus' birth. A common language, Greek, would be used to spread the gospel message throughout the Roman Empire. Safe transportation routes throughout the empire would be used as Jesus' followers traveled and told the world about the good news of Jesus Christ.

Questions

1. List three characteristics of the Greek empire.
2. What difficulties did the Jews face when the Seleucids instead of the Ptolemaics took control of Palestine?
3. How was God's timing for Christ's coming perfect?

2 Politics and Geography in Palestine

Matthew 2

The area of Palestine was only about 150 miles (241.4 km) from north to south and 50 miles (80.5 km) from east to west. Although Palestine was small, its impact on the world was great. The continents of Asia, Europe, and Africa merge in the area around Palestine. Trade routes crisscrossed this tiny strip of land to link Asia Minor and Egypt. Later, Greeks and Romans would use these roads to link their empires. Access to the Great Sea, as the Mediterranean Sea was called, also brought trade and commerce to Palestine.

Palestine was divided into three main regions. To the north was Galilee. Like the rest of Palestine, Galilee contained a number of geographical features within a small area. The deserts on the border gave way to fertile land and beautiful hillsides. The Jews living in Galilee were separated from the main group of Jews living to the south by Samaria. Because of this separation, Galileans tended to be independent and interacted with Gentiles. Jews living in Jerusalem were suspicious of Jews living in Galilee.

Herod the Great's fortress.

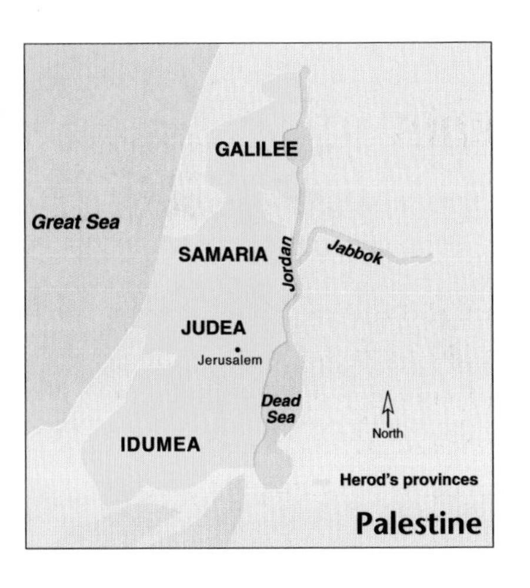

Samaria separated the Jews in Galilee from those living in Judea. As you may remember from your Old Testament study, the Jews despised the Samaritans. They thought of these people as neither Jew nor Gentile. The Samaritans were descended from the people that the Assyrians brought in to repopulate the land after Israel was exiled, along with the Israelites who were left behind. The Jews also disliked the Samaritans because they had interfered with the rebuilding of the temple and Jerusalem's walls. Jews continued to despise the Samaritans into Jesus' day.

The third region of Palestine was Judea, which was located in the south. Judea was the largest of the three areas in Palestine and included the city of Jerusalem. Jerusalem was the most important city in the world as far as the Jews were concerned. It was the city of David and the site of God's temple.

When Palestine was established as a Roman province, Hyrcanus, a Maccabean, was appointed king, but the power behind the throne was a man named Antipater. During Hyrcanus's rule, Herod, the son of Antipater, became ruler of Galilee. Eventually Herod also became king of Judea and became known as Herod the Great. Herod the Great was a ruthless man who would do anything to maintain his power. This extended to killing family members if he thought they were plotting against him. Herod the Great, who remained king until about the time of Jesus' birth, ordered the killing of all male children under the age of two in the area of Bethlehem. He did this in an attempt to rid himself of the threat of another potential king.

After Herod's death, the rule of Palestine passed to his sons. One son, Herod Antipas, ruled over Galilee. He was the king who ordered John the Baptist beheaded. Pilate sent Jesus to Herod Antipas during Jesus' nighttime trial. Herod the Great's other son, Archelaus, was made governor of Judea and Samaria after his father's death. Mary and Joseph avoided this king when they left Egypt and settled in

Nazareth. Even though the family of Herod the Great seemed to rule in Palestine, there was no doubt that the real power was the Roman Empire.

Questions

1. What were the three regions in Palestine? Describe each region.
2. Why did the Jewish people dislike the Samaritans?
3. After reading Matthew 2, provide examples of Herod the Great and his sons' impact on the story of Christ's birth and the decisions that Mary and Joseph made.

3 Religious Groups in Palestine

Matthew 16:1–12

You may be surprised to learn that at Jesus' time more Jews were scattered throughout the Roman Empire than were living in Palestine. For example, forty percent of the people living in Alexandria, Egypt, were of Jewish descent. One of the ways that these Jewish people remained united in their faith and traditions was through meeting at synagogues. Synagogues—places for corporate worship, prayer, and teaching—were first formed during the Jewish exile as a way to retain Jewish culture, traditions, and religion. For Jews living inside and outside of Palestine, the synagogue served to unite them in their cities and towns.

Jews living in Palestine were governed not only by the Romans and by Herod's family but also by the Sanhedrin. The Sanhedrin was composed of 70 Jewish elders who were given authority over religious matters among the Jews. Occasionally kings and governors would give the Sanhedrin additional power. The Sadducees and the Pharisees were the two religious groups within the Sanhedrin.

The Sadducees took their name from the high priest Zadok, who served at the time of David. As high priests, the Sadducees were responsible for Jewish relations with the Romans. Aristocratic, wealthy Jews joined the priests in being Sadducees. Since many of the Sadducees were priests, they favored the way in which the priests interpreted the law. The Sadducees saw the Pentateuch as being of greater

An Essene settlement and the Qumran caves.

importance than the rest of the Old Testament. They accepted only the written Torah and not the added laws and interpretations that came after it was written. Although the Sadducees were influential with Herod and Rome, they were not influential among their own people. When the temple was destroyed in A.D. 70, the Sadducees became irrelevant. They may have also been destroyed at that time.

The name Pharisee means "separatist." The Pharisees may have gained this name from their detractors or from the fact that they wanted to separate themselves from worldly practices. While the Sadducees worked to keep the sacrificial laws, the Pharisees worked to obey the letter of the laws. The Pharisees made and passed down a rigid code of laws based on their interpretation of the Scriptures. The Pharisees were popular with the people and often served as leaders in the synagogues. During Roman rule their political influence waned. The Pharisees remained as religious leaders even after the destruction of the temple, because their movement was not tied to temple sacrifices.

Among the Sanhedrin were scribes. The scribes studied and taught the law; they also interpreted the law and the teachings of other Jewish scholars. Both the Pharisees and the Sadducees had scribes in their group.

A variety of other Jewish religious groups were active at the time of Christ's ministry. Some of these included the Zealots, who wanted to break free from Rome. Many Zealots came from the province of Galilee and would later lead revolts against Rome. Another separatist religious group was the Essenes. These people chose to live apart from society. They hoped to establish a new covenant with God in their community.

Throughout his ministry Jesus had contact with these various religious groups. He frequently encountered the Pharisees and the Sadducees.

Questions

1. Why was the synagogue important to Jewish life?
2. Briefly describe the various members of the Sanhedrin and their beliefs.
3. What warnings did Jesus give his disciples concerning the Pharisees and the Sadducees (Matthew 16)?

4 The New Testament

Hebrews 8

The Bible, God's holy Word, is divided into many separate books. These books are grouped into two volumes: the Old Testament and the New Testament. You know from your past study of the Bible that the Old Testament recorded God's creation, humanity's fall into sin, and God's promise to send a Savior who would save his people from their sins. The New Testament focuses on God's fulfillment of his promise to send a Savior. The books of the New Testament explain the life, death, and resurrection of Jesus Christ and our relationship with him. The New Testament records the words of Jesus and of his disciples and the early church leaders who followed him.

The authors of the New Testament were all Jews, with the exception of Luke. Matthew, John, and Peter, three of Jesus' disciples, wrote books included in the New Testament. Other writers of the New Testament were individuals active in the early church and the spread of the gospel message. Only Luke and Paul did not directly witness Jesus' ministry.

The Nativity **by Correggio, 1530.**

The first five books of the New Testament are historical in nature. The Gospels, the first four books, focus on the ministry and life of Jesus. They are followed by the Book of Acts, which records the spread of the gospel message and the growth of the early church. The historical books are followed by a series of letters written to specific churches and individuals. Those written to specific churches are known as doctrinal letters and include the books of Romans and Colossians. Letters to individuals are classified as personal letters and include 1 and 2 Timothy and 1, 2, and 3 John. The lines between letters classified as doctrinal and personal are not always clear.

The first letters recorded in the New Testament belong to Paul. They are followed by the Book of Hebrews, whose author is unknown, and letters from a variety of other authors, including Peter and John.

The final section of the New Testament is that of prophecy, contained in Revelation.

All the books of the New Testament appear to be written from A.D. 50–100. Most Christians in the first century would have read the books in Greek, because Hebrew and Aramaic were not spoken outside of Palestine. The order in which the books appear in the Bible doesn't reflect the order in which they were written. James and Galatians were most likely the earliest writings.

In A.D. 367 Athanasius, the bishop of Alexandria, set the date of Easter and the 27 books that he accepted as the New Testament. Approximately 30 years later the Synod of Carthage ratified the list of New Testament books proposed by Athanasius. With few exceptions, these 27 books have remained the canon of the Christian church since that time. From the early days of the church the New Testament was translated into other languages to help spread the gospel. By A.D. 500 the New Testament had been translated into Latin, Syriac, Armenian, and Ethiopian. Christians continue to translate the New Testament today so that people from the ends of the earth can read and hear the gospel message of Jesus Christ.

Questions

1. Describe the divisions of the New Testament books.
2. Why do you think that most of the New Testament books were written between A.D. 50–100?
3. If Jesus was the fulfillment of the Old Testament, why do Christians still need to read it?

5 The Gospels

Matthew 8:1–4, Mark 1:40–45, Luke 5:12–16

Unlike some religious leaders, Jesus did not leave behind a collection of writings outlining his ministry and his expectations for his followers. Instead, the first four books of the New Testament give slightly differing accounts of Jesus and his ministry. These four books cannot be classified as biographies, because we learn little about Jesus' early life, appearance, or family. The books of Matthew, Mark, Luke, and John could be better considered as testimonies from those who followed Jesus; they speak of who he was and what he did in the short time he was on earth.

These first four books of the New Testament are commonly referred to as Gospels. The word *gospel* means "good news." The Gospels record the good news of Jesus Christ and were written at the time that the first generation who knew Christ was dying (A.D. 50–100). Each Gospel was written for a specific audience and has its own view of Jesus and his ministry. The Gospel writers selected which events of Jesus' ministry to include in their works, for it was impossible to include all that Jesus said and did. The various Gospels give us four different pictures of Jesus so that we can better know our Lord and Savior. John explains the purpose for writing his Gospel: "these are written that you may believe that Jesus is the Christ, the Son of God, and that by believing you may have life in his name" (John 20:31).

St. Matthew **by Ghiberti, 1419.**

The books of Matthew, Mark, and Luke are known as the Synoptic Gospels. These three Gospels contain a common view of Jesus' life and ministry. Often these books contain similar stories from Jesus' ministry explained in slightly different ways. Most scholars agree that the Gospel of Mark was probably written first. Matthew and Luke appear to have drawn on Mark's account in writing their Gospels. Some scholars believe that a collection of Jesus' sayings also circulated among the early Christians. This collection is known as Q, and scholars say that Q has since been lost. The Synoptic Gospels may also have been based on an oral tradition that missionaries presented as they brought the gospel from Jerusalem to the ends of the earth. (Jesus taught in such a way that his followers would be able to remember his words. One of techniques Jesus used was the telling of parables.) The Gospel of John was the last Gospel to be written. Whereas the other Gospels present a portrait of Jesus, John concentrated on the mind of Christ.

All of the Gospels were written in Greek, which was the universal language of the time. Jesus, however, spoke in Aramaic, which was the language of the people living in Palestine. The Gospel writers translated Jesus' words into Greek, although some of the Aramaic nuances remain.

The Gospel writers didn't use a smooth narrative style as they wrote. Instead, they included a variety of episodes from the life of Christ. These episodes were then placed in a historical context for readers. The divinely inspired authors wisely included the historical setting so that many years later, as we read the Bible, we can better understand Jesus' teachings.

Questions

1. How do the Gospel writings differ from a biography or a history textbook?
2. The Gospel writers did not include many historical details. Why do you think they chose to write from a large historical perspective instead of a minute one?
3. The greatest portion of the Gospels focuses on the last week in Jesus' life. Why?

The Synoptic Gospels

1 The Gospel of Mark

Mark 1:1–13

Tradition identifies John Mark as the writer of the Gospel of Mark. John Mark appears to have belonged to a wealthy Jerusalem family. His mother, Mary, was a friend of the apostles and may have provided the room for the Last Supper. Mary's home may have later become the center of the Jerusalem church. Although Mark may not have witnessed all of the events in his Gospel, he saw some of them. Mark was familiar with the leaders of the early church. He accompanied Paul and Barnabas on part of their first missionary journey. The Bible records that for unknown reasons Mark left the missionaries and returned home. Paul's initial disgust with Mark was later changed to admiration for this dedicated Christian.

Mark's Gospel is closely associated with Peter's preaching. Peter's speech at Cornelius's home (Acts 10:34–43) appears to be the outline for Mark's Gospel. Mark may have heard Peter preach many times and may have drawn his writing from those sermons. Early Christian tradition speaks of Mark recording Peter's words in his Gospel.

People gathered here to watch the chariot races; the fire started in this neighborhood.

The Gospel of Mark was

probably written during the time of persecution under Nero. When Rome burned to the ground in A.D. 64, Nero blamed the devastation on the Christians. Peter and Paul are assumed to have been martyred by the Romans during this time. Mark's Gospel shows the audience a suffering Jesus. The Gospel makes no secret of the fact that anyone who follows Jesus must "deny himself and take up his cross and follow me" (Mark 8:34). The first hearers of the Gospel of Mark would have been attuned to Jesus' suffering and that of his followers.

Mark's book is the shortest Gospel. His writing style is concise and factual, a style that would appeal to the Roman mind. Mark's accounts of Jesus' ministry are brief and active. Throughout the Gospel he keeps the action moving forward, almost at breakneck pace. Forty-two times words similar to "immediately" are used as he moves from one scene to the next. The reader follows Jesus' ministry through its various locations to its end in Jerusalem.

While Mark's Gospel moves quickly from one event to the next, he seemed to have kept in mind that many readers or hearers would not be familiar with Jesus or his ministry. The Gospel centers on Jesus' identity and provides meaningful episodes explaining who Jesus is. Jesus' miracles are given a prominent place in Mark's account. Mark also paid particular attention to those unfamiliar with Jewish life. Whenever Mark mentioned Jewish law, he fully explained its significance to his audience. Mark also took care in translating Aramaic words for his audience.

Questions

1. Describe John Mark's background.
2. What are some of the characteristics of Mark's Gospel?
3. How may have events in Rome affected Mark's Gospel?

2 A Different Kind of Leader

Mark 1:14—4:34

From the opening verses, Mark's Gospel makes it clear that Jesus is the Son of God. Mark describes people who were unsure of who Jesus was. Disciples, priests, and crowds all questioned Jesus' identity. After Jesus calmed the Sea of Galilee, the disciples asked, "Who is this? Even the wind and the waves obey him!" (Mark 4:41). The questions that the various people asked only confirmed what Mark said from the beginning: Jesus is the Son of God, the promised Messiah.

Mark's Gospel does not describe Jesus as referring to himself as the Messiah. Instead, Jesus hid his identity. For example, after healing a man with leprosy, Jesus instructed him not to tell others about the event. One reason that Jesus may have made this request is that he knew he had a long ministry ahead of him and the time had not yet come for his death. Jesus also knew that if he became known as a healer, people might miss his message. Instead of coming to hear his teachings, the people would gather to be healed of their illnesses.

The Sea of Galilee.

Jesus further obscured his identity by referring to himself as the Son of Man rather than the Son of God. Once again we note that in the opening verse of Mark, Jesus is referred to as God's Son, a description that leaves no doubt about his identity. The first example of Jesus referring to himself as the Son of Man occurs in the story of the paralytic whose friends lowered him from the roof in order to be healed. The Jewish leaders criticized Jesus for forgiving the man's sins. Jesus explained to the leaders that "the Son of Man has authority on earth to forgive sins" (Mark 2:10). Jesus' adoption of the title Son of Man has its roots in the Old Testament Book of Daniel. In one of Daniel's visions he saw "one like a son of man, coming with the clouds of heaven. . . . He was given authority, glory and sovereign power; all peoples, nations and men of every language worshiped him. His dominion is an everlasting dominion that will not pass away, and his kingdom is one that will never be destroyed" (Daniel 7:13–14). It is also interesting to note that others did not refer to Jesus as the Son of Man; it was a title that he reserved for himself. If Jesus had referred to himself as the Messiah, he would have increased the expectations of the people for a ruler who would lead a rebellion against the Romans and establish a kingdom on earth.

Jesus further baffled expectations by the people he associated with. Jesus chose ordinary people like fishermen to join him as disciples. He also chose a tax collector, a person disdained by many Jews. Jesus spent time with the weak and the outcasts of society. The Jewish leaders would at times see Jesus' interactions with unclean and immoral people as scandalous. From the beginning of his ministry, Jesus illustrated that he would be a different type of leader. Jesus' ministry would be a living picture of the gospel he preached. The message of the gospel is for all people, whether they immediately identify him or not.

Questions

1. Mark's Gospel provides many examples of people not knowing who Jesus was. How do their questions help us to learn about and understand Jesus?
2. How did the Son of Man embody the characteristics described in Daniel 7:13–14?
3. How was Jesus' leadership style different from the people's expectations of the promised Messiah?

3 A Time of Popularity

Mark 6:30–56

Mark 6 focuses on a time of popularity in Jesus' ministry. The chapter opens with story of Jesus' rejection by people in Nazareth. You may have heard the phrase "a prophet is without honor in his hometown." This phrase has its origins in Jesus' words to his disciples as he left Nazareth. We can understand why those with whom Jesus had grown up may have found it hard to believe that he was the promised Messiah. After all, they had known him from the time he was a baby, and he had played with them or their children. The people in Nazareth had the opportunity to experience firsthand Jesus' ministry and healing, but they chose instead to criticize him.

Mark 7 begins with another example of people criticizing Jesus' ministry. In this case Jesus faced opposition from the Pharisees. They spent a great deal of time and energy looking for ways to undermine Jesus. Between these two episodes of criticism, Mark sandwiches examples of how Jesus was embraced by the people with whom he ministered and healed.

Bethsaida is the possible location of the feeding of the 5,000.

Evidence of Jesus' popularity is presented in the story of the feeding of the 5,000. What we might not initially recognize is that Jesus fed far more than 5,000 people. The number 5,000 included only the men who were present, and many women and children also followed Jesus. The setting was a remote place along the shores of the Sea of Galilee. The people were so eager to hear the gospel message that they followed Jesus on shore to where his boat would eventually dock. Mark tells us that Jesus "had compassion on them, because they were like sheep without a shepherd" (Mark 6:34). The image of a sheep and a shepherd is common throughout the Bible. Ezekiel 34—an entire chapter—explores the image of shepherds and sheep. The chapter concludes with God placing his claim as the shepherd of his sheep, "You my sheep, the sheep of my pasture, are people, and I am your God, declares the Sovereign Lord" (Ezekiel 34:31).

Additional Old Testament images occur in the way the people were arranged as they waited for their food. They sat in groups of hundreds and fifties, which served as a reminder of the way that Moses had arranged the Israelite camp in the desert. The miracle of the five loaves and two fishes may also have reminded people of the way that God provided manna for the people in the desert. Jesus is often referred to as the bread of life. Since we know the story of Jesus' death and resurrection, we also know that the way in which Jesus gave thanks and broke the loaves foreshadowed the Last Supper. Jesus' miraculous meal was not finished when the people were fed. It extended to the disciples collecting 12 baskets of leftovers. For the Jewish people the number 12 would immediately remind them of the 12 tribes of Israel and God's faithfulness to them.

The crowds following Jesus went to great lengths to be near him. They followed him to a remote area without even thinking about their need for food. The wilderness, a place without food, became an oasis when Jesus was there. Jesus was the people's source of physical nourishment, and more importantly, he satisfied their souls as well.

Questions

1. What Old Testament connections can be made in the story of the feeding of the 5,000?
2. What questions did people pose about Jesus' identity in Mark 6?
3. Mark used contrasting viewpoints to present the episodes he chose from the life of Jesus. In Mark 6, how did the author show the human and divine viewpoints?

4 The Challenges of Discipleship

Mark 8:27—10:31

For much of Mark we have heard people ask, "Who is this man, Jesus?" Only as Jesus prepared for his final journey to Jerusalem do we learn from Mark the repeated answers to that question. The first answer occurs when Jesus asked the disciples who people thought he was. After they responded with answers such as Elijah or John the Baptist, Jesus then asked who the disciples believed him to be. Peter's resounding answer was, "You are the Christ." The use of the word *Christ* is important in that Jesus never used the title himself. He knew that for the Jewish people the name *Christ* implied that he had come to save them from the Romans and establish an earthly kingdom.

It's also interesting that the disciples cited Elijah and John the Baptist as possibilities for Jesus' identity. The people seemed more willing to think that Elijah or John the Baptist could be brought back to life rather than that the Messiah was present with them! You may also remember that Herod had heard about Jesus and wondered whether Elijah or John the Baptist, whom he had beheaded, had returned from the dead.

In the events on the Mount of Transfiguration we find another reference to Elijah. He along with Moses joined Jesus and appeared before Jesus' three closest disciples—Peter, James, and John.

Mount Tabor, the traditional site of the transfiguration.

Mountains had been places where Elijah and Moses had experienced God's presence. These two prominent individuals from the Old Testament had made many sacrifices in their efforts to follow God and lead his people. Jesus' suffering and death would bring about salvation for these two giants of the faith as well.

As at Jesus' baptism, God the Father spoke at the transfiguration. As in the time of Moses, God spoke from a cloud. He confirmed for the three disciples that Jesus was his Son and that they were to listen to him. In the end, the transfiguration showed Jesus as he would be after his suffering, death, and resurrection. Jesus would once again be united in glory with his Father.

Elijah's return seems to be a frequent theme in passages from Mark. The disciples raised questions of Elijah's importance following the transfiguration, when they asked, "Why do the teachers of the law say that Elijah must come first?" (Mark 9:11). The background for their questions is Malachi 4:5, where the prophet stated, "See, I will send you the prophet Elijah before that great and dreadful day of the Lord comes." The disciples and other Jews expected that Elijah would return before the promised Messiah. What they failed to recognize was that John the Baptist's ministry paralleled that of Elijah. Both men prophesied to kings and queens who rejected their message. Jezebel was Elijah's nemesis, while Herod and Herodias tried to silence John the Baptist's message. Both prophets brought a message of repentance and spoke God's truth even if it brought personal danger. Elijah's message had come again through the words and actions of John the Baptist. There was no need to look for the coming Messiah because he was already present and among them.

Questions

1. What was the confusion surrounding the return of Elijah?
2. In Mark 8:27—10:31, what examples do you find of Jesus' order being different from the way in which the world is ordered?
3. Jesus' disciples had many opportunities to ask him questions. List two questions that you would have liked to ask Jesus if you had been one of his disciples.

5 The Gospel of Matthew

Matthew 1:1–17

From the earliest years of the church, the Gospel of Matthew has been ascribed to Jesus' disciple Matthew Levi. You may remember that Matthew worked as a tax collector before following Jesus. Scholars generally agree that Matthew's Gospel was written after the Gospel of Mark. About 80 percent of Mark is included in Matthew's Gospel. Scholars disagree about the exact date of Matthew's composition. Some place it before the destruction of Jerusalem because there is no reference to that significant event. Others place it after A.D. 70 and the destruction of Jerusalem at the hands of the Romans.

The Gospel of Matthew was particularly suited for churches familiar with Judaism. In fact, Matthew is the only Gospel that uses the word *church*. Matthew refers to God's covenant with Abraham and Jesus' fulfillment of that covenant. The opening chapters of Matthew repeat the refrain "that it might be fulfilled" in citing how Jesus came as the fulfillment of promises that God made in the Old Testament. On 65 occasions Matthew refers to Old Testament passages. Jesus' ministry as recorded in Matthew is shown in the light of the Old Testament, but Matthew makes it clear that Jesus came to save the Gentiles as well.

From the opening verses of Matthew, Jesus is shown as the fulfillment of all that God promised in the Old Testament. Matthew's opening verses echo the frequent listing of generations contained in Genesis

Earlier versions of Old Testament writings, used heavily by Matthew, were discovered here in the Qumran caves.

and throughout the Old Testament. Jesus' lineage is traced back to Abraham, the father of Israel. The initial verse of Matthew also indicates that Jesus descended from David's line. Jesus would fulfill the promise that David's royal line would rule forever. The lineage that Matthew uses traces Jesus' ancestry through Mary's husband, Joseph. Other Old Testament genealogies trace children through their father. By tracing Jesus' ancestry through Joseph, Matthew follows the Old Testament tradition. The family tree of Jesus makes his Jewish heritage indisputable. The genealogy puts to rest any argument that the events in Matthew are mythological. Jesus was a living, breathing human who was part of an earthly family.

Another characteristic of Matthew is the design of the book. Matthew's Gospel revolves around five main discourses. Your study of Matthew will focus on these five sections. Each of these discourses concludes with the phrase "when Jesus finished." These five sections may mirror the five books of the Pentateuch. Matthew shows that Jesus was the fulfillment of the Old Testament law. By using five key sections, he may have been pointing out that fulfillment.

Throughout the Gospel, Matthew acts as a rabbi patiently teaching his audience. He lingers over events that he may have thought his readers needed extra time to understand. He carefully explains those events or phrases that we might not understand on our own. Matthew's Gospel clearly illustrates that Jesus came to earth to save Jews and Gentiles.

Questions

1. How is the Book of Matthew arranged?
2. Find one passage in Matthew that refers to the church. What is the context in which the word is used?
3. Why does Matthew make such a point of Jesus being the fulfillment of the Old Testament?

6 The Sermon on the Mount

Matthew 5–7

The first of the five great discourses in Matthew is the Sermon on the Mount. The three sections included in this discourse are the Beatitudes, Jesus' ethical admonitions, and Jesus' teachings in contrast to those of the Jewish leaders. There is some question among scholars about whether Matthew may have compiled material from beyond the Sermon on the Mount to include in this section.

Matthew's Gospel makes it clear that Jesus fulfilled or brought to completion what was written in the Old Testament. Jesus articulated this when he said, "Do not think that I have come to abolish the Law or the Prophets; I have not come to abolish them but to fulfill them" (Matthew 5:17). In his teachings Jesus showed that his view of the law was far different from that of the Jewish leaders. Over time, God's original commands and laws had been added to by the scribes. The laws that had been added and passed on through tradition had undermined God's commands. In fact, some of the Jewish laws diminished those found in the Old Testament. Some of the specifics concerning the law had been reworked so that if a person was attentive to the details, he or she could obey the law perfectly. By manipulating the laws so they could be obeyed completely, the scribes took away the mystery of God's grace. Part of the purpose of the law was to illustrate for us how great our sins are and how much we

Mount Beatitudes, where Jesus may have preached the Sermon on the Mount. Notice the lilies of the field.

need a Savior. Only through God's grace can we be saved and not by any ability to perfectly obey his commands.

Jesus' explanation of the law far exceeded any expectations the Jewish leaders had of the people. Jesus separated himself from the legalistic interpretation of the scribes and Pharisees. Jesus contrasted the Pharisees' view of the law with the true interpretation that God had intended. Jesus deepened the law and its meaning for those who heard. It was not enough that a person did not murder. A person remaining angry with another was committing the same sin in a different way. No longer could those who truly followed God get by with sinful behavior because it did not specifically break a law. Instead, Jesus showed that a new attitude was needed in keeping God's commands.

Jesus also spoke of dealing swiftly and completely with sin. One of the techniques that Jesus used in presenting this material was hyperbole. Hyperbole is a literary technique in which intentional exaggeration is used to emphasize a point that a person is trying to make. For example, when Jesus spoke of adultery he stated, "If your right eye causes you to sin, gouge it out and throw it away. It is better for you to lose one part of your body than for your whole body to be thrown into hell" (Matthew 5:29). Jesus' point was not that we physically harm ourselves but that we take our sins seriously.

The teachings of the Sermon on the Mount do far more than point out the greatness of our sins. Jesus also provided strategies for how we are to deal with our sins. One of these is that we reconcile ourselves to others with whom we disagree. Jesus also taught that oaths are not necessary if we are guided by speaking only the truth. Jesus also explained the correct way in which to worship God through prayer, offerings, and fastings. Jesus presented a template for his followers to use in the words of the Lord's Prayer.

A final theme in the Sermon on the Mount is the rewards of discipleship. Jesus did not hide the difficulties of following him. He didn't make obeying God's laws any easier for the people, but those who accepted him and sought to follow his commands would one day be rewarded. The last Beatitude recorded in Matthew makes clear the cost and the rewards of following Christ. "Blessed are you when people insult you, persecute you and falsely say all kinds of evil against you because of me. Rejoice and be glad, because great is your reward in heaven, for in the same way they persecuted the prophets who were before you" (Matthew 5:11–12).

Questions

1. How did Jesus' explanation of the law differ from that of the Jewish leaders?
2. What is hyperbole? How did Jesus use this technique in Matthew 5–7?
3. Look over the Beatitudes. How do they explain that being a follower of Christ means acting in ways that are either active or passive?

7 The Mission

Matthew 10:5–42

We often think of the disciples after Pentecost going out and preaching the Gospel of Christ, but this is a misperception. Even before Jesus' death, resurrection, and ascension, the disciples had been sent out by Christ to bring his message to others. The second major discourse in the Gospel of Matthew focuses on Jesus' message to his disciples before he sent them out to preach to the Jewish people in Palestine.

The disciples weren't completely prepared for their first missionary journey. They hadn't yet seen how Jesus would suffer and die for their sins. Jesus empowered his disciples as they set out on their first missionary journey. He told them to cast our demons and heal the sick in his name. He also alluded to the work of the Holy Spirit in Matthew 10:19–20: "But when they arrest you, do not worry about what to say or how to say it. At that time you will be given what to say, for it will not be you speaking, but the Spirit of your Father speaking through you." By sending the disciples, Jesus taught them that his work could be performed by others in his name. After Jesus' ascension, the apostles would work tirelessly in carrying his message to the nations. Even though the disciples were not completely prepared, they willingly carried out the work Jesus had called them to do.

Christ Praying, **artist unknown.**

The Kingdom of Heaven

Throughout the Synoptic Gospels the phrase "the kingdom of heaven" or "kingdom of God" is used. These two phrases express the same idea. Matthew's Gospel uses the phrase "the kingdom of heaven." One reason for this was that Matthew was writing for a primarily Jewish audience. Devout Jews would not use the name of God. By referring to the kingdom of heaven, Matthew was showing respect for his Jewish audience.

Some people confuse the kingdom of heaven as meaning the kingdom in heaven. At the time of Jesus' ministry, many Jews thought that he would bring about an earthly kingdom. Neither of these two views expresses what the phrase "the kingdom of heaven" or "kingdom of God" means. Jesus' kingdom would not be temporal but rather eternal. Similarly Jesus' rule would not be confined to heaven but extend throughout the universe.

Jesus' coming to earth signaled the presence of his kingdom. John Timmer, in *Four-Dimensional Jesus: Seeing Jesus through the Eyes of Matthew, Mark, Luke, and John* (Grand Rapids, Mich.: Faith Alive Christian Resources, 2001), explains the kingdom as "what life on earth would be like if God were King. It is our world as God envisions it and as God is making it" (page 42). Jesus' ministry made the kingdom of God a reality then, now, and in the future.

Jesus often explained his kingdom metaphorically. These metaphors helped to connect his kingdom with things familiar to his disciples. Some of these comparisons included mustard seeds, yeast, and nets. Through these metaphors Jesus helped his listeners understand not only the kingdom but also the responsibility of kingdom membership. Being a resident of Christ's kingdom demands uncompromising, obedient service to him.

Jesus didn't send out his disciples with any illusions about how their message would be met. Some people would embrace the message that the disciples preached. They would open up their homes to the disciples and care for their needs. Jesus told his disciples to take nothing with them for their journey. They would depend on those who accepted what they said in the name of Christ.

Others would reject the message. Jesus told the disciples to shake the dust off their feet as they left homes or towns where Jesus was rejected. This was a sign that Jewish people used to indicate the town or home was unclean. Those who rejected the gospel message were unclean in the eyes of God.

Jesus also explained that in the name of Christ, the disciples would be faced with arrest, persecution, and even death. Once again Jesus made it clear that following him involved a cost. The disciples were encouraged to stand firm in the face of persecution. God had great rewards for those who believed in his Son, but those would come later. The Bible does not give us any indication that the disciples faced any persecution on this first missionary journey. Jesus' words about persecution would have greater meaning for the disciples later. They would also ring true with Matthew's audience, which faced immense persecution at the hands of the Romans.

This discourse ends with Jesus telling his disciples, "If anyone gives even a cup of cold water to one of these little ones because he is my disciple, I tell you the truth, he will certainly not lose his reward" (Matthew 10:42). Jesus concluded by reminding his disciples that they were to care for fellow believers. As Jesus' followers faced persecution, it would be especially important for them to care for one another and to remind one another of the rewards that Christ had in store for them.

Questions

1. What did Jesus mean when he told his disciples to "be as shrewd as snakes and as innocent as doves" (Matthew 10:16)?
2. Compare Luke 14:26–27 with Matthew 10:37–39. What message did Jesus give his followers that was presented in two different ways?
3. Why do you think so much of Matthew 10 is spent with Jesus explaining the cost of bringing his message to the world?

8 Parables

Matthew 13:1–52

You may have heard parables described as "earthly stories with heavenly meanings." This definition simplifies the complexity of Jesus' teachings. Jesus' parables often spoke of the kingdom of heaven, which is not clearly visible or understood by us. The kingdom of God that Jesus spoke about was not confined to heaven. The parables connected abstract concepts such as the kingdom of heaven with known images. The images helped in drawing comparisons between God's world and ours. There were heavenly themes in the parables, but they were themes that primarily had implications for the world in which we live.

Another frequent misconception about the parables is that they are allegories. Allegories are extended metaphors in which objects, people, and actions represent one thing in the guise of another. An allegory has a dual purpose. The first is in the events, characters, and setting of the story, and the other is the ideas that they meant to convey. For example, in the parable of the mustard seed, a person may say that the seed equals Jesus' message and the mustard tree stands for the kingdom that Jesus' message establishes. This may appear to be a possible interpretation, but it is not the only one. Such a single interpretation minimizes the impact of the parable. An allegorical interpretation doesn't take into account the action or setting of the parable. Allegorical understandings may ignore connections that the parable may have with Old Testament images or the events surrounding the presentation of the parable. In addition, we do not get a sense of the parable as a whole. Although some of

A pearl.

Jesus' parables may fit under the category of allegory, not all of them do.

Parables can also come in different literary forms. Some parables are simple metaphors or similes. Others are extended stories that may include allegorical elements. Whatever the form, parables are united in their use of analogies. Some parables make use of multiple analogies. Parables can also include protagonists and antagonists that force us to take sides as the parable is told.

Another characteristic of Jesus' parables is repetition of form or themes. Parables frequently contain twists and turns that we may not expect. These unexpected turns force us to pay attention and take a second look at Jesus' words.

Literary scholars like to say that good metaphors have inexhaustible explanations. For example, to say that a 16-year-old is like a 2-year-old may seem like an insult to the 16-year-old! But if you think about the comparison a little more, you will see that there are many other explanations. Two-year-olds are learning to walk, run, and be independent. Two-year-olds frequently say, "I can do it myself." Sixteen-year-olds are also gaining more independence through learning to drive, staying out late, and having jobs. Sixteen-year-olds are learning to provide for themselves and don't always care to hear parental advice.

Like a good metaphor, parables have multiple themes and meanings. As our lives change and our faith grows, the significance of certain parables may shift and change for us as well. While the nuances of a parable may change with time, the central themes of the parables remain those that Jesus taught.

Questions

1. What is an allegory? What is the problem with interpreting parables as only allegories?
2. Why did Jesus use parables to teach the people? (See Matthew 13:13–17, 33–35.)
3. The parables in Matthew generally follow the form of a simile. Locate two other parables in the Gospels that follow different literary forms.

9 Church Order

Matthew 18

The fourth discourse in Matthew focuses on how Jesus' kingdom community is to be different from that of the world. The context in which Jesus spoke was a discussion among the disciples about who would be the greatest in the kingdom of God. Jesus did not begin with a long, theoretical discussion. Instead, he used an object lesson to illustrate what it means to be great in his kingdom. Jesus called a child to him and explained that in order to become great in his kingdom, a person needs to become like a child. Like the child in Jesus' illustrations, we need to come to Jesus when he calls. We are not to linger. Jesus also explained that we are to humble ourselves like a child. We are not to get caught up in our abilities or greatness. Like a child, we are to be trusting. We know the trust that a child has for his or her parents to care for his or her spiritually, physically, and emotionally. In the same way we are to put our trust in God alone. It is important that we do not equate becoming like a child with childlike faith. Our faith should continue to mature while our attitude remains that of a trusting, humble child.

Sheep.

Jesus was not finished with the illustration of the child in teaching what it means to be a member of his kingdom. In his teachings we are also instructed in how the body of Christ, the church, is to operate. Immediately after speaking of becoming like children, Jesus gave a sharp warning. Under no circumstances are believers to lead others astray. We have a responsibility as members of the body of Christ to uphold others in the faith. Jesus spoke passionately that it would be better for a person who leads others to sin "to have a large millstone hung around his neck and to be drowned in the depths of the sea" (Matthew 18:6). Jesus emphasized his warning with another strong statement: "If your hand or your foot causes you to sin, cut it off and throw it away. It is better for you to enter life maimed or crippled than to have two hands or two feet and be thrown into eternal fire" (Matthew 18:8). We know that Jesus' statements were not to be taken literally. What they do is show how seriously we are to take sin and our responsibility not to lead others into sin.

Jesus' discourse in Matthew 18 makes it clear that greatness in the kingdom of God is far different from what the disciples expected. It involves humbling oneself before God and trusting in him completely. It also requires care for other believers. The parable of the lost sheep illustrates the responsibility for fellow Christians to seek out those who have strayed from Christ. Matthew's account of the parable indicates that the lost sheep in this story is a member of those believing in Christ. Luke's Gospel provides a twist on this parable. In Luke 15:1–7 Jesus states that the sheep who was lost was an unbeliever. Both parables of lost sheep illustrate the responsibility of the body of believers to protect the weakest of believers as well as to search out those who do not believe.

Jesus made it clear that membership among the body of believers is to be far different from that found among other communities of people. Members of Christ's body are responsible for one another. They will look out for the needs of others. They will confront sin and be willing to forgive those who sin against them. Members in Christ's kingdom are to model themselves after their head, Christ.

Questions

1. Why are Christ's followers to become like children?
2. How are the members of Christ's kingdom to be characterized?
3. How are the members of Christ's body to respond to those who have sinned against them (see Matthew 18:15–20)?

10 Eschatology

Matthew 24:1—25:46

Matthew's five discourses are arranged in chiastic structure. You may remember from your study of the Old Testament story of the tower of Babel that a chiasm is a literary device in which the parts are balanced against one another. Matthew's opening discourse is one of blessing focusing on the Sermon on the Mount. This is followed by a discourse of instruction outlining Christ's mission. The central discourse explains the kingdom of God to Jesus' followers through the use of parables. The fourth discourse parallels that of the second discourse in giving the disciples additional instruction. The fifth and final discourse serves as a contrasting balance to the first in listing blessings for those who have accepted Christ and curses for those who have not.

In looking at this final discourse of Matthew, it's important for us to consider the context in which Jesus spoke. On Palm Sunday the crowds had cheered Jesus' arrival in Jerusalem. The plot against Jesus would be explained in the opening verses of the following chapter. These chapters come as Jesus left the temple for the last

Remains of the Roman destruction of Jerusalem in A.D. 70.

Eschatology

The term *eschatology* refers to the biblical view of events that will take place when Christ returns. The root comes from the Greek word *eschatos,* which means "last." Biblical eschatology is not limited to the New Testament. The Old Testament prophets preached of God's judgment and promises for the unrighteous and the righteous. The prophets preached that God would continue to rule history and events until the last days. Often in the Old Testament the phrase "the day of the Lord" was used to speak of these last days. In many respects, these references pointed to the time of Christ's birth and ministry. At other times the prophecies reached beyond Christ's initial time on earth to the time he will return in glory. The future that the Old Testament prophets referred to focused on the future of the nation of Israel.

Christ Healing the Withered Hand **by James J. Tissot, 1836–1902.**

There are many different types of eschatology in the New Testament. The first is realized or present eschatology. This refers to the time of Jesus' initial coming and ministry. Then there is future eschatology, looking to the time in which Christ returns in glory. Along with these two types are general and personal eschatology. General eschatology refers to those events of the end times that will happen to all people. Personal eschatology focuses on the events that will happen to each person, righteous or unrighteous, at the time of Christ's return.

Eschatology is not an easy subject to discuss. Jesus says that "no one knows about that day or hour, not even the angels in heaven, nor the Son, but only the Father" (Matthew 24:36). Christians differ in their understanding of the signs of the end times and the events preceding Christ's return. All, however, agree that Jesus will come again.

time. What we are given in Matthew 24–25 are the last scenes before Jesus' arrest. Jesus' disciples approached him privately to ask about the end times and the day of his coming. The disciples had just drawn Jesus' attention to the beautiful temple in Jerusalem. Jesus took this opportunity to speak to them about the destruction of the temple and Jerusalem as well as his coming. At times it is difficult to discern when Jesus was speaking about the temple's destruction and when Jesus was calling attention to his second coming.

In A.D. 70, not even 40 years after Jesus' crucifixion, the city of Jerusalem and the temple were destroyed by the Romans. The historian Josephus described the destruction and the fleeing people in a way similar to Jesus' words in Matthew 24. Jesus told his disciples that "not one stone here will be left on another; every one will be thrown down" (Matthew 24:2). Jesus was not using abstract language to describe the destruction of the temple. What he said literally came true when the Romans under Titus sieged and eventually destroyed Jerusalem. Jesus connected the eventual destruction of the temple and Jerusalem to his return. Just as Jerusalem and the temple would pass away, so will this world.

Although Jesus gave the disciples some of the signs of his return, he did not indicate that his return was imminent. Many of the descriptions Jesus used had their roots in the Old Testament. Symbols of great suffering, darkness, blood, fire, and smoke were reminders of Old Testament events and prophecy. Many of Jesus' descriptions reminded people of the sinful time preceding the flood, the wicked cities of Sodom and Gomorrah, and the plagues that fell upon Egypt.

Prophetic imagery from Joel, Isaiah, and Ezekiel also found its way into Jesus' descriptions.

Jesus issued a warning to his disciples about the signs of the end times. He warned them to be careful of false signs and the misreading of the signs. Following the warning, Jesus presented the disciples with three parables. They spoke of the end times, but their emphasis was on how the followers of Jesus were to act until he came again. Jesus took his time with these parables. Unlike some of Jesus' other teachings, these were not concise. Jesus made sure that his disciples understood what was expected of them in his absence. They were not to idly await his return. They were to use this time productively while always being prepared for his coming.

Questions

1. Define chiasm and explain how Matthew used this structure in his writing.
2. Explain in detail how Jesus used one of the Old Testament stories or prophecies in his explanation of the signs of his coming or the destruction of Jerusalem and the temple.
3. What are we to do as we await Christ's second coming?

11 The Gospel of Luke

Luke 1:1–4

The Gospel of Luke is the most literary of the three Synoptic Gospels. Four songs or poems are included in the opening chapters of Luke. Like any good storyteller, Luke sets his story in a time and place, in this case, the context of historical events in the Roman Empire. Luke's presentation of the Gospel of Jesus is also well-written and organized. He includes rich details about the setting and people that bring the stories to life.

Baptism of Christ **by Leonardo Da Vinci, 1470.**

From the early days of the church, Luke has been accepted as the author of the Gospel bearing his name. He was most likely a Gentile physician who was educated in the Greek manner. He served as a friend and companion to Paul on his missionary journeys. Luke wrote his Gospel account from those who had witnessed the events in Jesus' life. Luke and Acts are considered companion books written by the same author.

As a Gentile, Luke had a unique perspective of Jesus' ministry. His writing shows a sensitivity to the Gentiles who would read or hear his Gospel account. Luke's account of Jesus' genealogy differs significantly from Matthew's record. Luke did not trace Jesus' ancestry to Abraham, the father of Israel. Instead, Luke mapped Jesus' genealogy to Adam, the father of all people, Jew and Gentile. Luke also provided accounts of Jesus' acceptance of all people. He included those people who would be considered distasteful to the Jews. Stories of Jesus' love for all people include the story of the good Samaritan and Jesus' stay with the tax collector Zacchaeus. Luke also differed with his account of Jesus' trial. For a Gentile, Jesus' trial before a Roman court would hold more significance than that before the Sanhedrin. Luke understood these differences and focused on Jesus' trial before Pilate. Luke's Gospel showed that Jesus had indeed made a place for Gentiles in his church.

Most importantly Luke understood the need for his audience to have a clear understanding of the way of salvation. Luke's Gospel begins with the announcement of John the Baptist's birth followed by that of Christ. From the beginning Luke presents Christ as fully God and fully man. Jesus was a perfect member of humanity. Luke carefully traces the development of Jesus' ministry from Galilee, to Judea, and finally to Jerusalem. Jesus patiently outlined his ministry to his disciples in increasing complexity through his time with them. Luke follows this same format as he records Jesus' ministry to his audience. Luke also explains for those unfamiliar with Palestine the importance of the various locations in which Jesus ministered. Luke's account of Jesus' ministry makes it clear that Jesus was not a threat to the Roman Empire. The revolution that Jesus started went far beyond the bounds of any earthly kingdom. Jesus' ministry would have eternal rather than temporal consequences.

A final in Luke's Gospel is the role of the Holy Spirit. In the early chapters of Luke we read that Zechariah was filled with the Holy Spirit at the naming of his son, John, and prophesied concerning his son's ministry and that of the one who would follow him. The Holy Spirit's presence at the beginning of Jesus' ministry is included in the account of Jesus' baptism and temptation in the wilderness. At the end of Luke, Jesus promised that this same Holy Spirit would fill his disciples. Luke also included Jesus' summary of the events that brought salvation and the need for the disciples to bring this message to all nations. "This is what is written: The Christ will suffer and rise from the dead on the third day, and repentance and forgiveness of sins will be preached in his name to all nations, beginning at Jerusalem. You are witnesses of these things. I am going to send you what my Father has promised; but stay in the city until you have been clothed with power from on high" (Luke 24:46–49). Luke's Gospel is filled with reminders that Jesus' message is for all people. The Holy Spirit was active in Jesus' life and ministry and would also be in the lives of those who followed him.

Questions

1. Describe the author of Luke.
2. What are some of the characteristics of the Gospel of Luke? How did Luke include Gentiles in his Gospel?
3. Page through the Book of Luke. Find three examples, not mentioned in the textbook, where Jesus showed compassion to people who might have been excluded from proper Jewish gatherings.

12 Preparation for Jesus' Birth

Luke 1:5–2

Angels played a prominent role in the days of the patriarchs and the exodus but seemed to have been largely silent for the duration of the Old Testament. We rarely read of angel visits or messages to God's people after the kingdom of Israel was established. The opening chapters of Luke, however, are filled with examples of angelic visits.

The first angelic visit was to Zechariah, an elderly priest, who was entrusted with the task of burning incense in the Holy Place of the temple. The angel Gabriel stunned Zechariah with his announcement that he and his barren wife would have a son who would be the forerunner to the Messiah. Zechariah seemed more surprised by the fact that he and his wife would have a child than that their son would prepare the world for the Messiah's ministry. Because of his unbelieving response, Zechariah was silenced until his son was named. When Zechariah showed that he believed God's plan by naming his son John, his voice returned. Luke is the only Gospel that includes details of the events surrounding the announcement and birth of John the Baptist. This fits with Luke's attention to the many people who were part of Jesus' life and ministry. Individuals such as Zechariah and Elizabeth are among the many that Luke describes.

***The Annunciation* by Fra Angelico, 1440.**

The next angelic appearance came to Mary. Luke's Gospel is unique in telling the story of Jesus' birth from his mother's perspective. The angel began with the same phrase that was used in the story of Zechariah: "Do not be afraid." Unlike Zechariah, Mary responded in faith. She trusted that God would work out the details of this unlikely event. Mary must have known that she would have faced condemnation for being pregnant before being married. In fact, she could have been stoned to death. But in childlike faith, Mary trusted that God would work out these difficulties as well.

While Jesus' birth was unassuming, the announcement of it was not. In grand style, the night sky opened and a company of angels announced the Messiah's arrival. Once again an angel prefaced God's great news with the phrase "Do not be afraid." The angel then announced the details of Christ's birth so that the shepherds knew exactly where they were to go to worship their Lord and Savior, now an infant. It is fitting that those who first knew of Jesus' birth were humble shepherds. The Old Testament often described God as a shepherd leading his people. Jesus would use this same imagery in his ministry as he described his relationship to the people. Jesus advocated childlike faith, and he preached to the common people of his day. We need only to think about how people may have responded if the King of kings had been born in Herod's palace and announced by heralds throughout the kingdom to realize the perfection of God's plan. God's Son had come to earth to save all people—poor and rich, Jew and Gentile, esteemed and overlooked, sick and healthy. All classes of people in Palestine would be touched by Jesus' ministry. The humble shepherds of Bethlehem, by carrying out their daily tasks, were honored by being the first to see the Son of God made flesh.

Questions

1. List two specific times that angels appeared in the Old Testament. How were these appearances significant?
2. List the people named in the opening chapters of Luke. Give a one-sentence description of each person.
3. Four songs or poems are recorded in the opening chapters of Luke. List these four songs or poems and explain when each was spoken or sung.

13 Ministry Preparations

Luke 3–4:5

Luke kept in front of his audience the events taking place at the time of Jesus' ministry. The Roman Empire was governed by Tiberius when Jesus began his ministry. Tiberius reigned from A.D. 14–37. Locally, Pontius Pilate served as the Roman governor of Judea. His rule lasted only 10 years, from A.D. 26–36, and coincided with Jesus' earthly ministry and death. Herod the Great died shortly after Jesus' birth, and one of his sons, Herod Antipas, ruled in Galilee. Herod Antipas was the ruler referred to as Herod throughout the three years of Jesus' ministry. By fixing the events taking place in the world, Luke made it clear to his audience that Jesus was fully human.

The Jewish people also had a high priest who served as their spiritual leader and intercessor with Rome. Only one high priest served in the temple at a time, so it's unusual that Luke would mention Annas and Caiphas as high priests. Annas served as high priest in Jerusalem from A.D. 6–15, until the Romans deposed him. He was followed as high priest by his sons as well as his son-in-law Caiphas. Caiphas served as high priest from A.D. 18–36. One of the reasons both men were listed as high priests may be that Annas continued to exert his influence over the high priests long after he had been removed from his position.

Bust of Emperor Tiberius.

Jesus' public ministry began when he was about 30 years. The vagueness of Jesus' age as recorded in Luke was typical of the time. Often people reading the Bible want to fix Jesus' age as exactly 30. Jesus may have been exactly 30, or he may have been 34. One of the difficulties in determining Jesus' age at the beginning of his ministry is that it's not entirely clear when he was born.

An additional problem for scholars comes in Luke's account of Jesus' genealogy. Luke's genealogy differs significantly from that of Matthew. One of the most striking ways is that Jesus' ancestors are traced back to Adam to show that Jesus came to save all people, not just the Jews. This genealogy is also interesting since Luke concludes not with Adam but God. Jesus' heavenly Father is included in this very earthly genealogy. Luke does not mention all of Jesus' ancestors. Instead, only the most notable persons are included, such as David, Jacob, Abraham, and Noah. Many scholars believe that Luke traced Jesus' ancestry through Mary. This would make sense because Mary was Jesus' blood relative while Joseph was his adoptive earthly father. Because Luke included a detailed account of Jesus' miraculous virgin birth, it would follow that he would take the unusual step of recording Jesus' lineage through Mary's family. Others wonder if Luke provided Joseph's actual genealogy while Matthew recorded the royal lineage of Christ. In either case, Luke reminds us of Jesus' humanity through the genealogical record.

Questions

1. What was happening in the Roman and Palestinian world at the time of Jesus' ministry?
2. How does Luke's genealogy of Jesus differ from that of Matthew?
3. How did John the Baptist prepare the people for Jesus' ministry?

14 Glimpses of Jesus' Ministry

Luke 7–9:50

Luke's Gospel lingers over the various people with whom Jesus interacted during his ministry. The passages in Luke 7–9 include several examples of extended character descriptions. By developing characters, Luke gives us insight into how Jesus cared for the diverse people who followed him.

The first example of an extended characterization occurs in Luke 7:1–10, with the story of the centurion from Capernaum whose servant was ill. From Luke's description we learn that the centurion was greatly loved and admired by the people of the city. Even though he was a Gentile, he had built a synagogue. His concern for his sick servant further illustrated the compassion that he had for those around him. One of the traits that separated the centurion from others who were following Jesus was his display of respect. He recognized Jesus' power and authority in ways that the Jews who followed Jesus did not. The centurion humbled himself before Jesus knowing that Jesus could heal his servant without even entering his home. Not only did Jesus heal the servant, but also he commended the faith of the centurion.

Another extended character description occurs in Luke 7:36–50. Here Luke describes a meal that Jesus shared with a Pharisee. An evening meal such as this one was an important event. People were seated according to the status that the host

Remains of a fourth century synagogue that was built over a first century synagogue.

deemed they possessed. From the rebuke Jesus later gave to Simon the Pharisee, we learn that Simon did not treat Jesus with respect or honor. Simon did not even provide the common courtesy of having Jesus' feet washed. Luke includes the details of Simon's inner thoughts, which Jesus knew. Luke's description shows that Simon was not so much interested in hosting Jesus as in trying to find a way to find fault with him.

The other critical character at Simon the Pharisee's home was an uninvited guest. Considering the number of people and servants who were present at the meal, it wouldn't be surprising for someone to come in from the outside. We know from Luke's description that this woman had led a sinful life. We also know from Luke's writing that Jesus most likely was reclined along a table, which was customary for that time. It's easy to imagine how the woman came up behind Jesus without being noticed and began to wash his feet. When Jesus was criticized by the Pharisee for allowing this type of a woman to touch him, Jesus told a parable. The parable made clear to the Pharisee and the woman Jesus' relationship with each of them.

Luke's characterizations enable us to gain a clearer picture into the types of people who interacted with Jesus throughout his ministry. All these people had a role in Christ's ministry and made a choice either to follow him or reject him.

Questions

1. What types of details did Luke include in his character descriptions?
2. What do you think accounted for John the Baptist sending his disciples to discover Jesus' identity? How did Jesus respond?
3. The record of Jesus' ministry includes three examples of people being raised from the dead. Two of those examples are found in Luke 7:11–16 and Luke 8:40–56. Briefly describe the circumstances surrounding how Jesus raised these two individuals from the dead.

15 Luke Writes about Jesus' Mission

Luke 10:25—11:13; 16; 18:1–30

This unit has introduced the different characteristics of the three Synoptic Gospels. Each Gospel differs slightly in its selection of events from Jesus' life, but they are unified in presenting Christ's message of salvation. Many of the Jewish leaders in Jesus' day found his message particularly difficult to understand. These leaders were not only skeptical about Jesus being the Messiah; they also failed to understand Jesus' message.

The story of the good Samaritan occurs only in the Gospel of Luke. Through this parable, Jesus again illustrated that he was a different type of teacher from those the people were used to hearing. Jesus' teachings showed that actions are more important than the definition of a word such as "neighbor." How God's law is brought to life in the actions of his people is more important than trying to obey each law perfectly. Showing love to others involves more than speaking about love or feeling the emotions associated with love. The parable of the good Samaritan shows that God's kingdom involves social justice as well. During his ministry, Jesus provided many examples of what it means to help the poor, sick, and hurting. His parable of the good Samaritan directed those who heard to follow the model of the righteous man in Jesus' story.

***The Merciful Samaritan* by Carl Julius Milde, 1803–1875.**

The parable of the good Samaritan arose from a question that an expert of the law presented. He asked the question not because he wanted an answer but because he was trying to trap Jesus. The expert broached the topic by asking Jesus what a person had to do to inherit eternal life. The expert didn't seem to understand that inheritance is generally not something that a person earns. Inheritance instead comes to a person because of his or her relationship with an individual. Jesus didn't answer the expert's questions directly. Instead, Jesus responded with a question for the expert, "What is written in the Law? . . . How do you read it?" (Luke 10:26). Jesus knew that that those who studied the law allowed for various interpretations within set boundaries.

The expert, feeling a need to save face, went on to ask another question after he had given the standard response from the law. This second question asked Jesus to define the word *neighbor.* Once again Jesus used an indirect response to the expert's question. This time Jesus answered with the parable of the good Samaritan. As the parable continued, the questioner may have anticipated that a member of his group would be the one to rescue the injured man. He must have been shocked and surprised to learn that the neighbor in the story was a Samaritan. Rather than tell the man who the neighbor was, Jesus asked the expert in the law to answer that question for himself. Since the Jewish people despised the Samaritans, it must have been especially difficult for the expert to say that the Samaritan had exhibited the qualities of a neighbor. This expert's response indicated how uncomfortable he was in giving the answer, "the one who had mercy on him." The expert's answer did not even include the ethnicity of the person who had been the neighbor. Instead, he refers to him as "one," trying to save face yet one more time in front of Jesus and his followers.

Questions

1. Why did Jesus tell the parable of the good Samaritan?
2. How did Jesus' teachings differ from what the expert in the law might have expected?
3. What are some of the other themes of Jesus' ministry in the passages that you read for today's lesson? Describe the situation in which each teaching arose.

The Gospel of John and Passion Week

1 Prologue to John

John 1:1–18

John's Gospel was written toward the end of the first century, around A.D. 90. Tradition holds that John, the last surviving disciple, wrote the book while living in Ephesus. The author of the Gospel does not refer to himself by name; instead, he assumes that his readers know his identity. He does refer to himself as the beloved disciple, and through deduction we can determine that this title belonged to John. The author of John was also familiar with Palestine and Jewish customs. The periodic use of "we" indicates that the author was an eyewitness to the events of Jesus' ministry.

The Gospel of John contains very little information from the Synoptic Gospels. Rather than repeat what was already known,

This gymnasium complex in Ephesus was dedicated to Domitian (A.D. 81–96).

A Biblical Who's Who

John was a poet, and he knew about words. He knew that all men and all women are mysteries known only to themselves until they speak a word that opens up the mystery. He knew that the words people speak have their life in them just as surely as they have their breath in them. He knew that the words people speak have dynamite in them and that a word may be all it takes to set somebody's heart on fire or break it in two. He knew that words break silence and that the word that is spoken is the word that is heard and may even be answered. And at the beginning of his Gospel he wrote a poem about the Word that God spoke.

Jesus, **artist unknown.**

When God speaks, things happen because the words of God aren't just as good as his deeds, they are his deeds. When God speaks his word, John says, creation happens and when God speaks to his creation, what comes out is not ancient Hebrew or the King James Version or a sentiment suitable for framing in the pastor's study. On the contrary. "The word became flesh," John says (1:14), and that means that when God wanted to say what God is all about and what man is all about and what life is all about, it wasn't a sound that emerged but a man. Jesus was his name. He was dynamite. He was the word of God.

Peculiar Treasures: A Biblical Who's Who by Frederick Buechner.
San Francisco: Harper and Row, 1979.

John provided new information. John did not write his Gospel for a certain culture or group of people. His Gospel was written for the church of all times and in all places. False teachings about Jesus' divine birth were circulating by the time that John wrote his Gospel. Some of Jesus' followers believed that God dwelt within Jesus from the time of his baptism until shortly before his crucifixion. Before and after these times, Jesus was human like everyone else. John disputed these teachings in his Gospel. From the opening verses John made Jesus' divine nature clear and unquestionable.

If dating John's Gospel to A.D. 90 is correct, the Gospel was written 20 years after the Roman destruction of the Jerusalem temple. This helps to explain John's attention in describing the temple rituals that Jesus came to fulfill. The division between the synagogue and the church also created struggles within the Jewish Christian community. This division assists us in understanding why John referred to Jesus' opposition as coming from "the Jews" rather than naming specific Jewish groups.

John expressed his purpose for writing the Gospel in the closing chapters. "But these are written that you may believe that Jesus is the Christ, the Son of God, and that by believing you may have life in his name (John 20:31). In this short verse the word *believe* is used twice. John used the word *believe* in his Gospel 98 times. Belief is not the only theme that John developed. His entire Gospel worked to illustrate Jesus' identity. The passages in John build on one another in showing Jesus' divine nature.

John also focused on Jesus' humanity. John's Gospel stressed the personal relationships that Jesus had with people. Unlike the other Gospel writers, John recorded no parables. Instead, he wrote lengthy passages describing Jesus' conversations with individuals. One example of such a conversation was recorded in Jesus' nighttime visit with Nicodemus. John's written account of this conversation contains the verse for which his Gospel is most famous: "For God so loved the world that he gave his one and only Son, that whoever believes in him shall not perish but have eternal life" (John 3:16).

Questions

1. What do we know about the author of John and when his Gospel was written?
2. What were some of the struggles of the early church that John addressed? What do you see as some of the struggles of today's church?
3. How does the quote from Frederick Buechner explain the significance of John's description of Jesus as "the Word"?

2 Jesus' Public Ministry Begins

John 1:19—4:54

From studying John's prologue, you learned some of the themes of his Gospel. These include that Jesus, and not John the Baptist, was the Messiah; Jesus was fully God and man; and Jesus called all people to believe in him. As John describes the beginning of Jesus' public ministry, these themes remain at the forefront.

Before Jesus began his public ministry, John the Baptist explained to the Jewish religious leaders that he was neither the Messiah nor the prophet Elijah. John indicated, through the words of Isaiah, that he was preparing the way for the Messiah. This dialogue was soon followed by Jesus' baptism by John the Baptist. When John the Baptist witnessed the Holy Spirit descending upon Jesus in the form of a dove, that sign confirmed for him Jesus' identity as the promised Messiah, the Son of God. Later John's Gospel will again record the testimony of John the Baptist. John the Baptist made it clear to those who questioned Jesus' identity that he was indeed God's promised Son.

Christ and the Woman of Samaria **by Anton Dorph, 1831–1914.**

John's description of Jesus' early ministry illustrates that Jesus was fully God and man. John records a number of significant miracles in Jesus' early ministry. Jesus' changing of water into wine at the wedding feast in Cana is generally regarded as his first miracle. John also records Jesus' healing of the official's son in Capernaum. We consider these events miracles, but John uses a different description. John refers to these events as signs. By calling them signs, John keeps the focus on Jesus, who performed the sign, rather than on the miracle. Each miracle served to point to Jesus' divine nature. John also uses the miracles as transitions between various themes in Christ's ministry.

Not all of the miracles that John records were dramatic. Some of the small miracles that Jesus performed might not be noticed initially. These include telling Nathanael where he was and what he had said before he met Jesus. Similarly, Jesus told the Samaritan woman details about her life that she had not revealed to him. These subtle miracles also serve as signs of Jesus' divine identity.

In the midst of these scenes from Jesus' ministry, John keeps in the forefront the fact that a person can only be saved by believing in Christ. Jesus' famous nighttime conversation with Nicodemus had at its center the theme of belief. Jesus took Nicodemus's beliefs in the teachings of the Old Testament and showed how these pertained to Christ's coming. Then Jesus told Nicodemus that only by believing in him could a person have eternal life. John the Baptist gave a similar message to his disciples: "Whoever believes in the Son [Jesus] has eternal life" (John 3:36). John even includes the Samaritans, those whom the Jews rejected, among those who heard Jesus' message and believed in him.

Questions

1. How was Jesus' identity clarified through John the Baptist?
2. Describe the types of people with whom Jesus interacted in the first four chapters of John. How did these different people respond to Jesus?
3. Compare and contrast Jesus' discussions with Nicodemus and the Samaritan woman.

3 Bread of Life

John 5:1—6:71

Apart from the resurrection story, the only miracle that is included in all four Gospels is the feeding of the 5,000. In John's account, Jesus asked his disciples how they should go about feeding this crowd gathered around them. Of course, Jesus did not need his disciples' input about how the crowd was to be fed. But Jesus' question did provide the setting in which the miracle would occur. Humanly speaking there was no realistic way for the disciples and Jesus to feed the huge crowd. It is notable that the crowd of 5,000 was counted by only the adult males present. Many women and children would also have been in the crowd. Using the food of the poor, fish and barley bread, Jesus fed the masses.

John also included the people's reaction to the miracle: they endorsed Jesus as a prophet like Moses. John pointed out throughout his Gospel that the faith of many people seemed to be tied to what they saw and experienced. Even after seeing Jesus' miracle, the people still didn't understand who he was. They associated him with Moses and the miracle of the manna. They also wanted to set him up as king. They tried to do this by force, but Jesus anticipated their actions and withdrew to a mountain.

***Miracle of the Loaves and Fishes* by James J. Tissot, 1836–1902**

In John's Gospel a miracle is typically followed by Jesus' teachings. Jesus acknowledged that the crowd had followed him not because of what they had heard but because of what they had eaten. They responded to Jesus' miraculous feeding by requesting another miracle under the guise that this would help them believe. They reminded Jesus of the miracle of manna in the desert. The crowd did not seem to equate the manna with God's provision for their ancestors in the wilderness. Instead, they seemed to see it as an easy way to gather food and gain time to pursue other interests.

Jesus pointed out that he was the bread of life. He was the provision that they needed for the wilderness times in their lives. Just as the manna came from heaven and the Father, so did Jesus, the bread of life. Jesus told the crowds, "I tell you the truth, unless you eat the flesh of the Son of Man and drink his blood, you have no life in you. Whoever eats my flesh and drinks my blood has eternal life, and I will raise him up at the last day" (John 6:53–54). The crowds following Jesus knew that body and blood are necessary for physical life. Christians would see that Christ's body and blood are necessary for eternal life with him.

The crowds did not understand Jesus' words as being connected with their spiritual well-being. Instead, they wanted a leader who could immediately provide for their physical needs and wants. As a result, many in the crowd rejected Jesus. They found Jesus' teachings hard to understand and were unwilling to remain with him. They may have thought that Jesus wanted them to physically eat his body and drink his blood. They failed to understand the spiritual aspects of his teachings. Even Jesus' closest disciples seemed unable to understand him. However, these disciples remained with him. Although they didn't necessarily understand Jesus' teachings, they believed in him and wanted to learn more.

Questions

1. Compare and contrast the crowd's reactions to Jesus at the beginning of Luke 6 and at the end of the chapter.
2. Read Luke 22:17–20, which is part of the account of the Last Supper. What similarities and differences do you see between Jesus' words at the Last Supper and when he taught the crowds that he was the bread of life?
3. How did the invalid at the pool called Bethseda ask Jesus to assist him? What did Jesus do instead?

4 The Christ

John 7:1—8:59

Jesus traveled to the Feast of Tabernacles sometime after it had begun. He knew that the Jewish religious leaders were waiting for his arrival so that they could take his life. John clearly states again that Jesus' time had not yet come. About midway through the festival, Jesus began preaching at the temple.

Even though he knew that the religious leaders wanted to take his life, Jesus did not back away from his message. Jesus used two prominent images from the Feast of Tabernacles as he preached to the pilgrims who had traveled to Jerusalem. On the final day of the feast, Jesus asked that all who were thirsty come to him. Throughout the week Jesus called to mind the water dedicated to God. Jesus' declaration of providing them with life-giving water should have reminded people of Isaiah's words, "The Lord will guide you always; he will satisfy your needs in a sun-scorched land and will strengthen your frame. You will be like a well-watered garden, like a spring whose waters never fail" (Isaiah 58:11). Jesus' words had a

A scene from Banyas—"Like a spring whose waters never fail."

The Feast of Tabernacles

The Feast of the Tabernacles was one of the feasts mentioned in the Pentateuch. The feast took place for eight days in late September–early October. The festival served as a harvest festival and as a reminder of Israel's desert wanderings. During the feast, people were to live in shelters made of branches. This would remind them of the tents that the people lived in as their ancestors wandered in the desert. Each day during the feast, water from the Pool of Siloam was offered to God. This reminded the people of God's provision of water in the desert. The second ritual took place at dusk, when four golden candelabra were lit. The lighting of candles symbolized the pillar of fire that God used to lead the people in the desert. Many Jewish pilgrims came to Jerusalem each year to attend this festival. They would pitch their tent shelters outside of Jerusalem.

profound effect not only on the people but also on the temple guards who had come to arrest him. Upon hearing Jesus' teachings, the temple guards went back to the priests and Pharisees empty-handed. One of the reasons they may not have arrested Jesus was their fear of the crowds who followed him. It is also clear that they were moved by Jesus' words and weren't prepared to arrest someone who taught with such authority.

Later Jesus would use another image from the Feast of Tabernacles. This time Jesus brought to mind the lighting ceremony, declaring, "I am the light of the world. Whoever follows me will never walk in darkness, but will have the light of life" (John 8:12). Jesus contrasted for the people the spiritual light of his ministry with the darkness of their beliefs and lives. Jesus' authority was placed in stark contrast with that of the Pharisees. After all, where had human interpretation of God's law brought them?

In the story of the adulteress, we see the authorities manipulating God's law to express what they wanted. The Pharisees unintentionally showed the people that there was no equity under the law. The woman was used as a way to try to trick Jesus. Her partner in adultery was not publicly humiliated. The Pharisees selected which sins they wanted to condemn, while Jesus condemned all sins. Jesus' words to the adulterous woman acknowledged not only her sin but also the grace that can be found in him.

Jesus clearly expressed his identity as God's Son. In contrast with the Jewish leaders, Jesus did not seek fame. Instead, he was motivated by doing God's will on earth. Jesus also shared the true reward that would come in serving him: life. Only those who followed the light of God's word would "never see death." The crowds may not have realized that Jesus' message went beyond the temporal and extended to the eternal.

Questions

1. Find additional Old Testament passages that refer to the coming Messiah as light and water.
2. How did plans for Jesus' arrest and death go wrong for the Jewish leaders (John 7–8)?
3. What was the connection between the living water of which Jesus spoke and the Holy Spirit?

5 The Rising Controversy

John 9:1—11:53

The Jewish leaders and rabbis continued to disapprove of Jesus' ministry despite the miracles and teachings that they witnessed. The Jews, as John referred to them, set their hearts and minds against Jesus and refused to change their opinions about him no matter what they saw or heard. Their disbelief seems especially unrealistic in view of the miracles Jesus that performed near the close of his public ministry. Even when confronted with the healing of the blind man and Lazarus's resurrection from the dead, they maintained that Jesus could not be the Son of God, the promised Messiah.

Jesus' healing of the man born blind brought immediate disapproval from the Jews because it took place on the Sabbath. Just as they had previously, the Jews clung to their Sabbath regulations and pointed to Jesus' miracle as a sin because of the day of the week on which it was performed. But the fact that Jesus healed the blind man on the Sabbath didn't keep others from identifying Jesus as sent from God. The Pharisees continued their investigation by questioning the healed man. With each question they asked, it became more apparent that Jesus was far more than a prophet or a miracle worker. The Pharisees went so far as to drag the man's frightened parents into the argument. They confirmed that he had been born blind, but they were afraid of providing any statement about who they thought Jesus was.

Reconstruction of the tomb of Lazarus.

John helps us to sense the Pharisees' frustration as they continued to question the man. Rather than create doubt, the interrogation served only to strengthen the faith of the man who had once been blind. Each time the Pharisees asked him a question, the title that he gave Jesus became greater. Initially the man called Jesus a prophet. Then he stated that Jesus was sent from God. Later he says that Jesus is one to whom God listens; finally he calls Jesus the Son of Man—Lord—and worships him. The story of the healing of the blind man is filled with irony. Although he was deprived of his sight for many years, his eyes and his faith became clear through Jesus. In contrast, the Jews who thought they would recognize and see the Messiah were filled with spiritual blindness. In the end the Jews rejected the blind man's testimony as well as Jesus.

The final miracle of Jesus' public ministry was the raising of Lazarus. Lazarus's resurrection was probably the most dramatic of all of Jesus' miracles. It also made the Jewish leaders more determined to see Jesus dead. Bethany was located about 2 miles (3 kilometers) from Jerusalem. News traveled quickly to Jerusalem of Lazarus's death and then of his miraculous resurrection at Jesus' command. The Sanhedrin quickly assembled to discuss this latest trouble that Jesus had caused. The Sanhedrin justified the actions that it later planned to take against Jesus by claiming it wanted to prevent a revolt against Rome. The Sanhedrin claimed to want to protect the people and nation from the trouble that Jesus could cause. At this point the high priest Caiaphas spoke to the assembly: "You do not realize that it is better for you that one man die for the people than that the whole nation perish." Caiaphas did not understand the deep spiritual truth of his words. Because of his disbelief, he was blind to the redeeming word of Christ.

Questions

1. How was Jesus' ministry different from that of the Jewish leaders and rabbis?
2. A number of Old Testament prophecies pointed to the Messiah as one who would open the eyes of the blind. Find two Old Testament passages containing these prophecies. Write out each one.
3. How did Lazarus's death and resurrection foreshadow Christ's?

6 Passion Week: The Triumphal Entry

Matthew 21:1–11; Mark 11:1–11; Luke 19:29–44; John 12:12–19

Up to this point, you have studied the ministry of Jesus by separately studying each of the Gospels. You learned characteristics of each Gospel and how individual authors revealed Jesus' life, ministry, and message of salvation. Approximately one-third of all the Gospels focuses on Jesus' final week in Jerusalem. The differing details of the Gospel writers provide us with a complete account of Jesus' words and actions in this most important week.

What we refer to as Passion Week coincided with the Jewish Passover celebration. Many pilgrims traveled to Jerusalem for the celebration. Jesus and his disciples were among this group. The Christian remembrance of Passion Week begins on Palm Sunday and concludes with Easter on the following Sunday.

The road from the Mount of Olives to Jerusalem.

Jesus and his disciples stayed in Bethany, where Lazarus had been raised from the dead, for Passover. On Palm Sunday, Jesus and his disciples traveled from Bethany through Bethphage and the Mount of Olives to Jerusalem. The trip through the Mount of Olives would have provided a spectacular view of Jerusalem and the temple.

Jesus took this journey into Jerusalem mounted on the colt of a donkey. The disciples brought this animal to Jesus just as he had instructed. The colt on which Jesus rode had never been used. Jewish sacrifices required that the animal used must be unblemished or unused. In selecting this mount, Jesus illustrated that his entry was for religious purposes and not political.

The reaction of the crowd contrasted with Jesus' purpose. The people threw their cloaks over the donkey and on the road. Their actions indicated the coming of royalty. Jesus rode into Jerusalem on a donkey much as his ancestor David had hundreds of years before. The crowd did not remember that humility and peace were also associated with the donkey. The crowd waved branches, including palm branches, as Jesus rode though the streets. The palm branches symbolized victory to the crowds gathered at Jesus' arrival. Palm branches were not native to Jerusalem, and people must have gathered them as they traveled through Jericho to celebrate the Passover.

When Jesus entered Jerusalem, his destination was different from what the people anticipated. Jesus did not go to the places of secular power. The purpose of his trip into Jerusalem was far greater than ridding Palestine of the Romans. Instead, Jesus went to the temple. He came to Jerusalem to do his Father's work and not the work of the people. The preparations for the Passover were underway in the temple area. The people were gathering unblemished lambs and preparing to make sacrifices for the celebration. Beginning with God's directions at the time of the exodus, Jewish people presented sacrifices to make them right with God. Jesus' arrival in Jerusalem signaled that the old system of sacrifices was about to change. The unblemished Son of God would be sacrificed once and for all, so that the people could be forgiven by God.

Questions

1. How did the crowds react to Jesus' entry? How did the Pharisees respond?
2. How did Jesus' entrance into Jerusalem fulfill Old Testament prophecies?
3. Many churches mark Palm Sunday by having children enter the sanctuary waving palm branches. How might this create some misperceptions regarding Jesus' triumphal entry?

7 Passion Week: The Temple

Matthew 21:12–17; Mark 11:15–19; Luke 19:45–48

The annual Passover celebration brought great crowds of Jews and Gentile believers to Jerusalem. The crowds were so large that the Mount of Olives was declared a part of Jerusalem to accommodate the visitors' desire to celebrate in the holy city. The Romans stationed in Jerusalem were on heightened alert during the Passover. They were on the lookout for any possible rebellion.

The temple at Jerusalem occupied about 35 acres and bustled with activity during Passover. Jews and believing Gentiles came to the temple to offer sacrifices and present their offerings. Rather than travel with sacrificial animals, the pilgrims bought them at the temple. Similarly the Passover pilgrims exchanged their money at the temple so that they would have coins free of human images for their offerings. The temple requirements provided a lucrative business for many people in Jerusalem. Money was to made from these traveling pilgrims as they bought their sacrificial animals and exchanged their coins. The exchange of animals and money occurred inside the temple in the Court of the Gentiles. This location easily accommodated all pilgrims.

Christ Driving Out Those That Bought and Sold by James J. Tissot, 1836–1902.

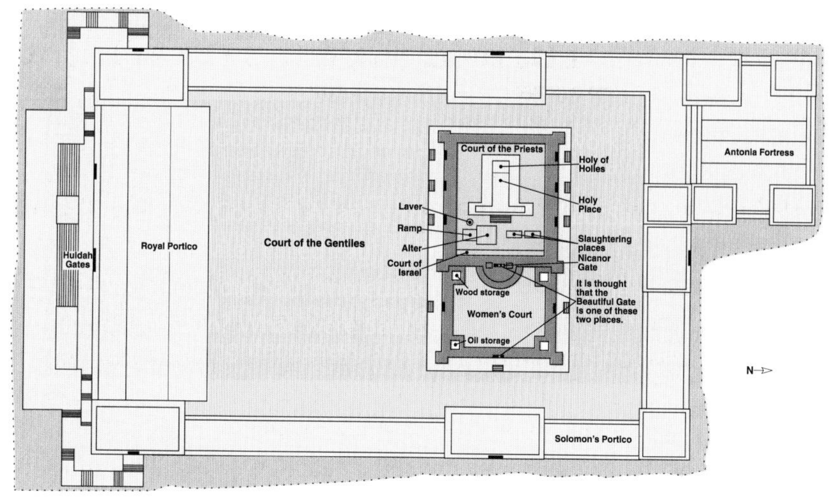

Herod's Temple

The Gentile court occupied the largest area in the temple. The Jews were taught that they were to be a light to the Gentiles, and this outer court enabled Gentile believers to worship in the temple, although they were not allowed to enter the other courts. By setting up stalls in the Gentile court, the Passover merchants made it nearly impossible for the Gentile pilgrims to pray and worship. This was the setting in which Jesus arrived on the day after his triumphal entry.

A first reading about the temple cleansing may lead us to understand that Jesus cleansed the temple because the merchants were not fair in their exchanges. When we look more closely, we learn that Jesus wanted all people to be able to worship in the temple. Luke says that Jesus cleansed the temple so that he would be able to preach. But there were other reasons for Jesus to cleanse the temple during this week.

Until this point in their history, the Jewish religious leaders' power to forgive sins came only through ritual sacrifices. The Jews were under the false assumption that their temple sacrifices provided them with a special relationship with God. Unfortunately for some, the power of these ritual sacrifices had usurped God's power.

In cleansing the temple, Jesus in essence destroyed the sacrificial worship at the temple. Jesus' death would make it unnecessary for sacrifices to be offered at the temple. Only through belief in

Christ can anyone be saved. Jesus' cleansing of the temple symbolized his destruction of the old order of things. His sacrifice on the cross would be once and for all people. Jews and Gentiles would be be able to come to God through him.

Questions

1. What Old Testament passages did Jesus quote as he cleansed the temple? What did these passages indicate to those who heard them?
2. How would Jesus' death on the cross make the temple and the sacrifices obsolete?
3. How did Jesus' cleansing of the temple attack the way of life of the Jewish leaders?

8 Passion Week: Preparations

Matthew 23:1–39, 26:1–16; Mark 12:38–43; 14:1–10; Luke 20:45–47; 22:1–6; John 12:2–8

The pilgrims in Jerusalem busily prepared for the Passover meal and celebration. Celebrants gathered what they needed for their meals of unleavened bread, lamb, and bitter herbs. Preparations were also being made for Jesus' death and crucifixion.

Jesus stayed in Bethany, which was a short distance from Jerusalem, during Passion Week. He stayed with his disciples and friends such as Mary, Martha, Lazarus, and others. Jesus also spent an evening at the home of Simon the leper, where a woman anointed him with expensive perfume. The Gospel accounts differ as to whether the woman anointed Jesus' head or poured the perfume on his feet. Whatever the case, the woman's gesture was extravagant. The disciples asked whether the money she spent on the perfume could not have been better given to the poor. It was customary during Passover week to present special offerings to the poor.

Celebrating Passover.

Jesus chastised the disciples for their criticism. He recognized the woman's gesture as an act of devotion to him. Jesus told his disciples that her actions were in preparation for his burial. Jews usually anointed a body with perfumes before burial. The exception came when the individual was put to death as a criminal. Jesus knew that he would die a criminal's death. The woman who anointed him had unknowingly made preparations for Jesus' death and burial.

Others were also involved making preparations for Jesus' death. The Jewish leaders continued to look for someone who would assist

Phylacteries

Phylacteries are two small boxes that Jewish men wear during morning prayer. Phylacteries are not worn during prayer on the Sabbath or during feast days. The two small boxes of the phylacteries are called the tefillin. The tefillin contain small scrolls with the words of Exodus 13:1–10, 11–16 and Deuteronomy 6:4–9 and 11:13–21. These four texts represent the Torah.

The tefillin are placed on leather straps and are then attached to the forehead and the upper arm. The practice comes from the literal application of Exodus 13:9, where, after Moses instructed the people, he said, "This observance will be for you like a sign on your hand and a reminder on your forehead that the law of the Lord is to be on your lips. For the Lord brought you out of Egypt with his mighty hand." The practice of wearing phylacteries appears to have begun sometime after the Babylonian exile. Some contemporary Jewish men continue to wear phylacteries during prayer.

Putting on phylacteries.

them in capturing Jesus while he was away from the crowds. After witnessing Jesus' anointing, Judas chose to hand over Jesus to the chief priests. We do not know what prompted Judas to betray Jesus. He may have been disillusioned that Jesus' mission did not include an earthly kingdom that would replace Rome. What the Bible does say is that "Satan entered Judas, called Iscariot, one of the Twelve" (Luke 22:3). The price that Judas and the chief priests agreed upon was 30 pieces of silver, about four months' pay for a worker. We also know from the Old Testament that 30 pieces of silver was the price of a slave.

For one week, the preparations for the Old Testament Passover celebration and its fulfillment in Jesus would overlap. Jesus, his disciples, and the pilgrims in Jerusalem had made their plans for the Passover meal. The preparations for Jesus' death had also been made. His body had been anointed for burial. Judas had conspired with the chief priests to hand him over. God's salvation foreshadowed in the Passover meal was about to be completed.

Questions

1. What preparations were made for Jesus' death?
2. The passages for this lesson are filled with people with contrasting reactions to Jesus' teachings. Write a short paragraph explaining some of their differing reactions.
3. Read the passages that are contained in the phylacteries. Write a brief summary of those passages.

9 Passion Week: Passover Supper

Matthew 26:17–56; Mark 14:12–52; Luke 22:7–53; John 13–14; 18:1–12

The Passover meal was the highlight of the festivities for the pilgrims in Jerusalem. Jesus and his disciples also held their Passover supper in Jerusalem. Despite the significance of the event, the disciples made no preparations for this meal of remembrance. Just as he had at Palm Sunday, Jesus directed his disciples in making preparations. The disciples were to look for a man carrying a jar of water. Carrying water was considered a woman's work, so it would not be difficult for the disciples to notice a man performing this task. Through this man, the disciples would be led to a home where they would celebrate the Passover. It is possible that Jesus made these arrangements ahead of time without the disciples' knowledge, because Jerusalem was crowded during the Passover. Some scholars think that the Passover was held in the upper room of the home of Mary, the mother of John Mark.

The Garden of Gethsemane with olive trees.

In the Middle East, eating with others was a gesture of friendship. Enemies would not eat with one another. Jesus knew of Judas' betrayal. Judas came to the Passover meal as Jesus' enemy. Jesus gave Judas every opportunity to change his mind and not betray his teacher. Jesus washed Judas' feet, just as he did for the rest of the disciples. He addressed Judas' betrayal in a subtle manner by identifying his betrayer with a piece of bread. The other disciples did not understand the significance of Jesus' offering Judas the first piece of bread. It was generally an honor to receive the first piece of Passover bread. Even at the moment of betrayal in the

Garden of Gethsemane, Jesus addressed Judas by saying, "Friend, do what you came for" (Matthew 26:50). Jesus gave Judas one last opportunity to turn from his plan, but Judas did not.

After celebrating the Passover, Jesus and his disciples walked to the Garden of Gethsemane, which was located on a lower slope of the Mount of Olives. Here Jesus prepared himself for the coming events of his betrayal, trial, and crucifixion. Jesus took three of his disciples—Peter, James, and John—with him some distance from the others. Jesus wanted his disciples to pray with him. He knew the temptations that they would face in the coming hours, days, and years. Jesus modeled for them the importance of prayer in trials and temptations. The disciples would share in Jesus' trials and sufferings, but they would also share in the glories of his rule in heaven.

Jesus knew in the Garden of Gethsemane the physical suffering that he would face on the cross. More importantly, Jesus would face the spiritual suffering of separation from God and the sins of all people placed upon him. Jesus prayed, "Father, if you are willing, take this cup from me" (Luke 22:42). We must be careful not to misunderstand Jesus' words. Jesus was not shirking responsibility. Instead, he was acknowledging the greatness of the task ahead of him while knowing there was no other way in which it could be accomplished. The second part of Jesus' prayer, "yet not my will, but yours be done" (Luke 22:42), reflects Jesus' willingness to do his Father's will above anything else. Jesus' prayer to his Father was of such an intensity that "his sweat was like drops of blood" (Luke 22:44). In contrast, his disciples slept.

Questions

1. What opportunities did Jesus give Judas to turn away from betraying him?
2. What temptations did the disciples face in the Garden of Gethsemane? How did they respond to these temptations?
3. How is Luke's chronology of the Passover meal different from that of Mark and Matthew? How is the material contained in John different from that in the Synoptic accounts?

10 Passion Week: Trial and Crucifixion

Matthew 27:35–60; Mark 15:24–46; Luke 23:33–54; John 19:18–42

After Jesus' arrest, he was led to the home of Annas. Annas had previously been a high priest, but the Romans had seen to it that he was deposed. Annas continued to work behind the scenes in the Sanhedrin. His son-in-law Caiaphas was now the high priest, and at one time or another all five of Annas's sons served as high priest.

Following Jesus' meeting with Annas, Jesus was taken to the home of the high priest, Caiaphas. You may remember that Caiaphas had said, "It is better for you that one man die for the people than that the whole nation perish" (John 11:49). It seems likely that Caiaphas questioned Jesus alone before the members of the Sanhedrin arrived.

The trial of Jesus by the Sanhedrin violated many Jewish laws. Trials such as this were not to be held at night with no witnesses for the defense. The witnesses that the Jewish council brought were unable to agree on their testimony. Jewish law dictated that

This Passion Week float depicts Jesus with Pontius Pilate on the left and a Roman soldier on the right.

Roman Crucifixion

We have some knowledge of crucifixion and can reconstruct the likely course of Jesus' last hours. Two further troublemakers, we are told, were also due to be killed. The three of them could be dealt with together. Whipped and beaten, already faint from loss of blood, condemned men were made to carry the wooden beams from which they would be hung. Mark tells how Jesus' cross was carried for him by Simon of Cyrene. . . . The victims were led to a bleak patch of rising ground outside the city's wall. Here was the regular site for executions. A series of posts stood out against the sky, eight feet high; into the top of each was cut a notch.

Jesus Dying on the Cross, **artist unknown.**

The routine was familiar. Nothing marked out this set of crucifixions from the last. Sometimes rope was used to fix the prisoner to the cross, sometimes nails. There is an ancient tradition that Jesus was nailed.

The beam was laid on the ground. The soldiers put Jesus onto his back across the beam and along it stretched out his arms. First one hand, and then the other: a soldier would press the back of Jesus' hand against the beam, hold a nail to the wrist, and drive it home, through pulse and bone, to the wood behind. The soldiers lifted the beam's ends onto two forked poles, hoisted the beam and Jesus into the air, and slotted the beams' center into the notch at the top of the post.

Now for the feet. Each of Jesus' ankles was sandwiched between a block of wood and the side of the upright post. From each side a nail was hammered in.

And there Jesus would hang, for as long as it took him to die.

It was an infamously, spectacularly cruel form of execution. It was used for rebels and runaway slaves. The longer they lasted, the better. A stool might be attached to the post, on which the victim could rest; his circulation would revive, his suffering would be prolonged. So much the better, too, that the mob could see what became of troublemakers: Here was a warning to anyone else who might dare oppose the might of Rome.

The Four Witnesses: The Rebel, the Rabbi, the Chronicler, and the Mystic
by Robin Griffith-Jones. SanFrancisco: HarperSanFrancisco, 2000.

the testimony of two witnesses must agree in order for an individual to be tried. The Sanhedrin twisted Jesus' words throughout this sham of a trial. Only when Jesus was put under oath did he confirm his identity as the Christ, the Son of God. The Sanhedrin immediately pronounced Jesus' death sentence. Once again this went against Jewish law, which stated they were to wait a day before announcing a sentence. Caiaphas had many powers as the high priest under Roman rule. However, he did not have the power to carry out executions. For this reason, Jesus was taken to the Roman procurator of Judea, Pontius Pilate.

Pilate became the procurator of Judea in A.D. 26 and remained in the position until A.D. 36. Pilate was responsible for Roman military and financial concerns in Judea along with appointing the high priest. Pilate often antagonized the Jews with his insensitivity to their religious laws. His plans to use the temple treasury to build aqueducts was met with great resistance. Pilate reacted to these uprisings or disagreements by excessive use of force. Eventually Pilate lost his position because of a blunder in dealing with the Samaritans and their religious practices.

The Sanhedrin brought Jesus to Pilate only because they needed his approval to carry out their death sentence against Jesus. The members of the Sanhedrin were eager for Jesus to appear before Pilate in his hall, but they would not enter it. If Jews entered the home of a Gentile, they would become ceremonially unclean. Pilate saw no reason for the sentence that the Sanhedrin had pronounced.

When he realized that Jesus was a Galilean, he sent him to Herod, who ruled that region.

Under cover of night, Jesus was then taken to Herod. Pilate did this more as a courtesy to Herod than for any other reason. The two men had long been enemies. Unwittingly the Sanhedrin had managed to bring Herod and Pilate, former enemies, together. This was the same Herod who had imprisoned John the Baptist and later ordered his beheading. Herod was more interested in seeing Jesus perform a miracle than he was in hearing the charges brought against him. Jesus performed no miracles for Herod, nor did Herod find any reason to have Jesus executed. Herod ordered that Jesus be mocked, beaten, and sent back to Pilate.

Pilate knew that Jesus was innocent. But he also knew that he could not afford to antagonize the Jewish leaders. The Jews then shouted the threatening words, "If you let this man go, you are no friend of Caesar. Anyone who claims to be a king opposes Caesar" (John 19:12). Hearing these words, Pilate made his decision. He could not allow even a whisper of opposition to Caesar reach Rome. The Sanhedrin bullied Pilate to get what they wanted. In the end, Pilate was more concerned with his own reputation and power than justice. Jesus, an innocent man, was condemned to die.

Questions

1. List the various trials of Jesus and who was present at each.
2. What motivated the Sanhedrin? How did this affect the way in which they tried Jesus?
3. What motivated Pilate? How did this affect the way in which he tried Jesus?

11 Passion Week: Resurrection

Matthew 28:1–15; Mark 16:1–13; Luke 24:1–49; John 20:1–30

The Gospel writers did not follow a single script as they wrote their accounts of Jesus. Each writer had a unique perspective on the events of Jesus' life and a particular audience in mind when writing about what he had seen or heard. Probably in no section of the Gospels is this more evident than in the telling of Jesus' resurrection. None of the Gospel writers dispute that Jesus rose from the dead on the first day of the week. They do differ in how individuals learned of Jesus' resurrection from the dead and responded to it.

The Gospel of Mark ends abruptly with the resurrection account. Three women walked to the tomb to complete the burial rituals that were hastily performed because of Sabbath observances. The women reached the tomb, found the stone rolled away, and heard an angel say that Jesus had risen. The women were to tell Jesus' disciples to go ahead to Galilee, where they would be met by their Lord.

Discipleship is one of the themes in the Gospel of Mark. The women were told exactly how to spread the news of Jesus' resurrection, but they failed to carry out the task. Mark provided examples throughout his book of the disciples' failure in following Jesus' commands. The women were to go to Galilee, where Jesus' ministry began. In the light of Jesus' resurrection, we are also to travel back to the beginning of

The Three Marys by Gaspako Lando.

Jesus' ministry in Galilee and retrace his steps so that we can more deeply understand his teachings.

Later manuscripts contain additions to Mark's Gospel that most Bible translations believe were not a part of the earliest manuscripts. Mark's abrupt ending may have reflected the speed in which he told the story. With Jesus' resurrection, all that Mark had spoken of in his Gospel had been completed. Or it is possible that he was forced to stop writing before he had finished. The ending to Mark's Gospel may have been lost. Some scholars see Mark's ending reflecting the time in which he lived. Jesus' followers were afraid in the days following his death and may not have been immediately eager to proclaim his resurrection.

Matthew changed and added details in his account that differentiate it from Mark's. Matthew's Gospel contains the witness of the guards who were posted at Jesus' tomb. These guards appeared before the Jewish leaders, where they were coerced into spreading the lie that Jesus' disciples had stolen his body. The guards' account of Jesus' resurrection would have been important to Matthew's Jewish audience. The guards confirmed that Jesus' resurrection involved his body and his spirit.

Luke's account of Jesus' resurrection shows him opening the minds and hearts of others to recognize him. Jesus was not immediately recognized in his resurrected body. On the Emmaus road, Jesus explained his identity to his fellow travelers by referring to Old Testament passages about the Messiah. Only when he revealed himself, did these disciples, and later others, see their risen Lord.

John's account contains other details about Jesus' resurrection. John described how he and Peter ran to the tomb only to find it empty. He also wrote of Jesus' conversation with Mary Magdalene in the garden. During this conversation, Jesus spoke of the uniqueness of his resurrected body. He was no longer limited by the confines of his earthly body. It is fitting that John recorded the conversation between Mary Magdalene and Jesus in the garden. In this garden, near the graves of the dead, Jesus' resurrection proved how he had conquered sin and death. The sins of Adam and Eve, and all people, in the Garden of Eden had been covered.

The early church did not rewrite the Gospels to make the writers perfectly agree. The church let the differences stand, thereby adding to the legitimacy of what was written. The accounts work together to provide indisputable evidence that Jesus had arisen from the dead. Through Christ's death we were brought forgiveness, and in his resurrection we receive new life.

Questions

1. How do the Gospels differ in their accounts of Jesus' resurrection?
2. On what details do the Gospel writers agree? Why is this important?
3. How did Jesus model how we are to be witnesses for him as he traveled with the two people on the way to Emmaus?

12 Ascension

Matthew 28:18–20; Mark 16:19–20; Luke 24:50–53

Forty days passed between Jesus' resurrection and his ascension into heaven. During that time, Jesus appeared frequently to his disciples. Because he was in his resurrected body, the disciples never knew when or where he would appear. We do know that most of those appearances came in Galilee. Jesus spent this time retraining his disciples. Only after his resurrection were the disciples able to reflect on Jesus' ministry and fully understand what he had taught them. Jesus helped them in this process as he explained again why he had come into the world. The disciples had seen the completion of Jesus' redeeming work and were being prepared to take this message to others. As Jesus taught them in Galilee, the disciples gained the strength and boldness that they would need for their future missionary work.

The Mount of Olives with a view of Gethsemane.

Jesus returned one more time to Jerusalem before his resurrection. Here he met his disciples and walked with them toward Bethany. According to tradition, Jesus stopped at the Mount of Olives, the site of his betrayal, to ascend into heaven. The Bible gives us no indication where Jesus ascended.

Jesus gave his disciples final instructions before he ascended to his Father. They were to bring his message of salvation to all nations. Jesus had primarily preached to the Jewish people before his resurrection. Now the gospel message was meant for all people —Jews and Gentiles. The disciples were to baptize the new believers in the name of the Father, Son, and Holy Spirit. Baptism serves as a sign that the individual belongs to Christ. Jesus concluded with words of comfort for his disciples. Even though they could no longer see his physical body, he remained with them. Earlier Jesus had told his disciples that all authority in heaven and on earth belonged to him. Jesus had proven this authority with his resurrection from the dead. Armed with this knowledge, the disciples could be sure that Jesus would be with them and empower them for the task ahead.

Jesus ascended into heaven to share God's glory. In heaven he would mediate on our behalf with his Father. Jesus' work on earth was completed; salvation had been won. But the work of the disciples had just begun. Following Jesus' ascension, the disciples returned to Jerusalem. They met daily at the temple to worship Christ. The temple had many smaller rooms where people could meet; the disciples and other followers of Christ probably met in one of these smaller rooms. The disciples remained in Jerusalem until Pentecost, when God would send the promised Holy Spirit.

Questions

1. What did Jesus do during the time between his resurrection and ascension?
2. Define the word *commission.* How did Jesus commission his disciples?
3. As Jesus' disciples, are we to travel to all nation to bring the Gospel?

Acts: To the Ends of the Earth

1 An Introduction to Acts

Acts 1

The Book of Acts serves as a companion to Luke's Gospel. Acts and Luke were addressed to Theophilus, who was most likely Luke's patron. The similarities in the writing style indicate that Luke and Acts were written by the same person. In Acts, Luke included precise details as he told the story of the early church. Many of Luke's details about specific locations have been confirmed by archaeological findings. When Luke inserted "we" in his narrative, we can assume that he was present at those events.

Scholars disagree about the time period in which Luke wrote Acts. Some scholars think that the book may have been written around A.D. 63, soon after the events in Acts took place, because the book includes no information about what happened to Paul after his two-year imprisonment in Rome. Luke also failed to mention the destruction of Jerusalem and the burning of Rome.

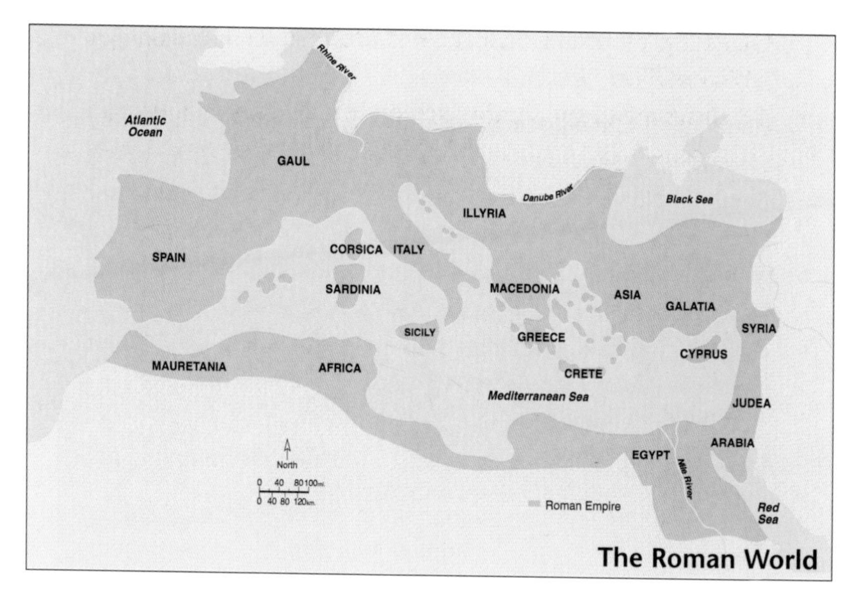

The Roman World

Disciple or Apostle?

A source of confusion for some people is why in Acts the twelve disciples are suddenly referred to as apostles. The word *apostle* is a Greek term used to identify someone who is an official representative of another. The representative is charged with carrying out a specific task or bringing a designated message. In contrast, a disciple is known as a student or a follower of a specific person or set of teachings.

When Christ was ministering on earth, his followers were r eferred to as disciples. Within Christ's group of followers was a special group of 12 people that he called to be his disciples. The number 12 corresponded to the 12 tribes of Israel. These 12 disciples followed Christ throughout his earthly ministry and did so at the sacrifice of finances, family, and friends.

***The Dispersion of the Apostles* by Charles Bleyre, 1806–1874**

The period of discipleship concluded with Christ's death, resurrection, and ascension. Before his ascension, Christ called his disciples to a new task. The disciples were to be directed by the Holy Spirit and preach Christ's gospel to all people. With a new mission, the 11 remaining disciples also gained a new title, apostles. Paul, who was not one of the 12, was also considered an apostle. Like the 12, he received a special call from Christ and dedicated his life to spreading the gospel message. Paul is considered the last of the chosen apostles.

Scholars who argue for a later date point out that Acts illustrates the spread of the gospel throughout the Roman world. They argue that the events in Jerusalem and Rome were not important in writing about the spread of the gospel.

Acts tells the story of the first 30 years of the church. Luke provided his audience with the historical foundation of Christianity and its spread throughout the Roman Empire. As is true for all historical documents, the time and place in which events occurred were critical in telling the story. The Book of Acts was structured according to Acts 1:8, where Jesus said to his disciples, "But you will receive power when the Holy Spirit comes on you; and you will be my witnesses in Jerusalem, and in all Judea and Samaria, and to the ends of the earth." Luke traced the geographical journey of Christ's message as told by his followers from Jerusalem, to Judea, Samaria, and finally Rome. The terms and descriptions used by Luke reflect the cultures and the people who encountered the gospel message.

Peter and Paul are the primary characters in Acts. The book includes lengthy speeches by each of these men, explaining the important themes of Christianity. Peter served as the leader in Jerusalem and later Palestine. Paul worked to spread the gospel outside the borders of Judea and Samaria. The information Luke gives about Paul's mission work provide a setting for the letters that Paul wrote to the early church. Paul's epistles immediately follow the Book of Acts.

Questions

1. What is the significance of the way in which Acts is organized?
2. What are some of the characteristics of Acts? How are these characteristics similar to those in the Gospel of Luke?
3. Why did the disciples choose a twelfth member? What criteria did they use to choose this new disciple?

2 Pentecost

Acts 2

Before his ascension, Jesus told the disciples to wait in Jerusalem for the coming of the Holy Spirit. The disciples followed Jesus' command even though they did not know when the Holy Spirit would descend. It is fitting that the Holy Spirit came ten days following Jesus' ascension on Pentecost. The Feast of Weeks, also known as Pentecost, was one of three Old Testament celebrations for which Jewish people traveled to Jerusalem to worship at the temple. Pentecost was a harvest festival that took place 50 days after Passover. While the Jewish people in Jerusalem were celebrating the harvest festival, the Holy Spirit prepared the disciples to gather God's harvest. Because those Jews gathered in Jerusalem came from around the world, the apostles were able to respond to Christ's commission by proclaiming the gospel to people from the ends of the earth.

The physical signs of the Holy Spirit's presence came in the "sound like the blowing of a violent wind. . . . They saw what seemed to be tongues of fire that separated and came to rest on each of

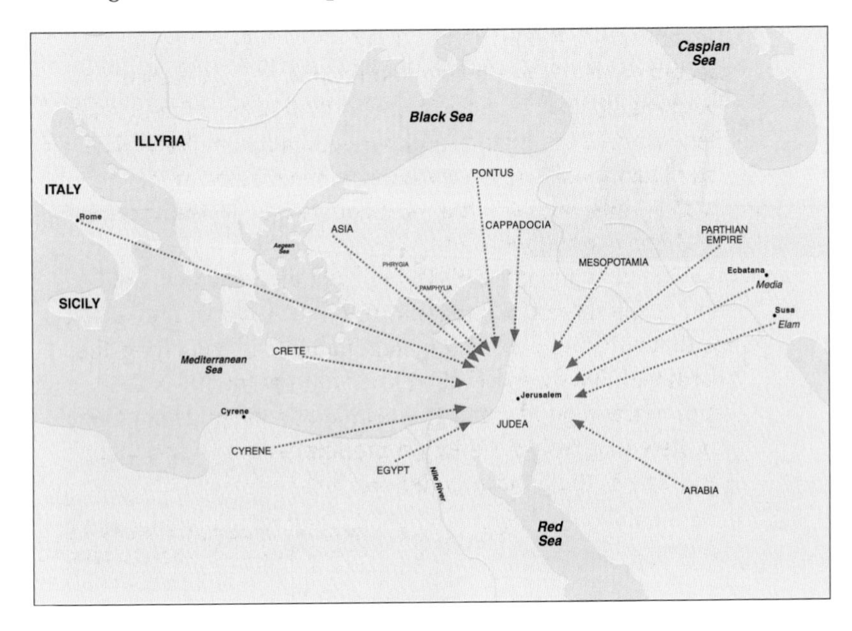

Doctrine of the Trinity

The doctrine of the Trinity can be difficult to understand. In the following passage from Kathleen Norris's *Amazing Grace: A Vocabulary of Faith*, the author writes about a friend who was having a difficult time believing that God could be three in one.

> Once a friend, a member of my small-town church, astonished me by confiding after worship that she no longer believed in the Trinity. . . . "I want one God," she said adding, "I know the Trinity is supposed to be one God, three in one. But I just can't believe it anymore."
>
> The first thing that popped into my mind was something I couldn't say out loud. It's the only phrase I recall from a lengthy Russian Orthodox meditation on the Trinity, that "outside the Trinity, there is only hell." For all I know, this may be true. But my friend didn't need to hear Christian theology expressed in such stark terms. I wondered if her anxiety might be a kind of hell; she attends church more faithfully than I but also seems to suffer more from a love-hate relationship with Christian faith. She told me that she had given up saying the Creed during worship, because it's all about the Trinity.
>
> It felt good to be talking hard-core theology after church; it doesn't happen often. "If you want completed, unadulterated monotheism," I said, "maybe you should become a Jew." "In western South Dakota?" she replied laughing. "It couldn't be any lonelier than being a Presbyterian Benedictine here," I said, and we both laughed. A few days later I happened across a metaphor for the Trinity, in Tertullian, of all people, arguably the most curmudgeonly theologian of all the curmudgeons of the early church. It's an image of the Trinity as a plant, with the Father as a deep root, the Son as the shoot that breaks forth into the world, the Spirit as that which spreads beauty and fragrance, "fructifying the earth with flower and fruit." I sent it to my friend, as she appreciates a good metaphor, and knows, deep down, that mystery is as real as the air we breathe, as everything that grows from the ground under our feet.

Amazing Grace: A Vocabulary of Faith by Kathleen Norris.
New York: Riverhead Books, 1998.

them" (Acts 2:2–3). You may find it interesting to learn that the word for "wind" in Hebrew is also used to mean "spirit." Just as it was fitting that the gift of the Holy Spirit came at Pentecost, it was also appropriate that what seemed to be tongues of fire came to rest on those who gathered. On that first Pentecost the Holy Spirit gave the apostles the courage, words, and languages so that they could preach to the crowd. The visitors' surprise at hearing the apostles speak in their own languages may have caused them to listen more closely to the message of Jesus Christ.

Pentecost **by Biotto Di Bondane, 1266–1337.**

When we think of the outpouring of the Holy Spirit, we often remember that the apostles were able to speak in languages that they had never studied. Sometimes we forget that the Holy Spirit also gave the once timid followers of Christ the courage and words to spread the gospel message to all who could hear. Equipped by the Holy Spirit, Peter preached to the crowd. He began by citing the Book of Joel as a way to explain the events that the crowd witnessed. He continued by proclaiming the life, death, and resurrection of Jesus. Finally, he called the crowd to repent and be baptized. In inviting them to be baptized, Peter was calling them to belief and a life of following Christ. The sermon format that Peter used on Pentecost would be followed by others as they preached the good news of Jesus Christ.

The Book of Acts is filled with references to the Holy Spirit. Luke's account of the early church makes it clear that the Holy Spirit was active in the lives of God's people. The Holy Spirit filled the believers with Jesus' promised power. The Holy Spirit also worked to provide unity among the believers. This core group of believers dedicated themselves to Jesus and all he had taught. Through the work of the Holy Spirit, God brought many people to salvation. The apostles' preaching, however, remained confined to Jerusalem and the surrounding area.

Questions

1. Why is it appropriate that the outpouring of the Holy Spirit took place on Pentecost?
2. Make an outline of Peter's speech. Other apostles would follow this same format when they preached.
3. What was Peter's purpose in citing the Old Testament quotations as he preached to the crowd?

3 Preaching in Jerusalem

Acts 3–6:7

You may remember from your study of the Gospels the important role that the Sanhedrin played in the lives of the Jewish people who were under Roman rule. The Romans granted the Sanhedrin limited authority over the Jewish people. The Sanhedrin's authority was primarily in the interpretation and application of Jewish religious laws. The high priest, approved by Rome, along with approximately 70 other leaders, served in the Sanhedrin. At the time of Pentecost, Caiaphas served as the approved high priest; however, his father-in-law, Annas, was recognized as the true high priest by the Jewish people.

Peter and John appeared before the Sanhedrin following the healing of a beggar at one of the temple gates. The members of the Sanhedrin knew that they faced a difficult task in trying to quiet the apostles and dismiss what they had done. Many people had witnessed the healing at the temple, and the Sanhedrin could not claim that the miracle was a trick. Later, when the Sanhedrin ordered the imprisonment of the apostles, an angel opened the doors and released them from the jail. Imagine the Jewish leaders' surprise the next morning when they found the apostles preaching at the temple rather than locked in a jail cell. Once again the apostles were forced to stand before the Sanhedrin.

The apostles, filled with Holy Spirit, were not intimidated by the Sanhedrin. They took every opportunity to preach the good news of Jesus Christ. The Sanhedrin did not argue with Peter when he spoke before them. They knew the role that they had played in

Solomon's Colonnade, where Peter addressed the onlookers after he healed the crippled man.

Jesus' crucifixion. They had tried to silence the stories of Jesus' resurrection. The members of the Sanhedrin were not interested in a debate with the apostles—they just wanted them to be quiet!

One of the characteristics of Acts is the inclusion of many speeches. Luke includes three speeches in recording the events of the Jerusalem church in Acts 3–6:7. Two of these speeches were given by Peter, but the third speech was given by a member of the Sanhedrin, Gamaliel. Gamaliel was a well-respected teacher who had instructed many of the leaders in the Jewish community. Much of the Book of Acts focuses on one of his students, Saul, who after his conversion became known as Paul. Gamaliel was a moderate member of the Sanhedrin. In his speech before the Sanhedrin, Gamaliel advised caution in dealing with the apostles. He reminded the Sanhedrin of fringe leaders who concerned them for a little while but soon fell out of favor with the people. He proposed that the apostles of Jesus might be another of these short-lived groups. As we look at the spread of the gospel message for the last 2,000 years, we see the truth in Gamaliel's closing words to the Sanhedrin: "I advise you: Leave these men alone! Let them go! For if their purpose or activity is of human origin, it will fail. But if it is from God, you will not be able to stop these men; you will only find yourselves fighting against God" (Acts 5:38–39).

Following Gamaliel's speech, the Sanhedrin ordered the apostles flogged, told them to stop preaching, and sent them home.
It appears that the Sanhedrin left the apostles alone for a short time. The apostles continued to preach despite the threats of the Sanhedrin, and more people were added to the number of believers. As the number of Christians increased, so did persecution by the Jewish leaders.

Questions

1. How did the Sanhedrin try to silence the gospel message?
2. How did Gamaliel's words prove to be prophetic?
3. What phrases are repeated in Peter's speeches in Acts 3–6:7? Why do you think these themes and phrases are repeated?

4 The Cost of Following Christ

Acts 6:8—8:3

Stephen was one of the seven people chosen to assist the apostles in ministering to the needs of the poor. After the apostles laid their hands on Stephen, the Holy Spirit filled him so that he was able to work miracles. The Holy Spirit also provided Stephen with boldness in preaching the gospel message of Christ. Stephen was reared a Hellenistic Jew, and it was to this group of Christian Jews that Stephen ministered.

The Hellenistic Jews in Jerusalem were unable to bring any legitimate charges against Stephen. Because of this, charges were made by false witnesses when Stephen was brought before the Sanhedrin. Stephen was accused of preaching against the law of Moses and saying that Jesus would destroy the temple. Jesus had also been brought before the Sanhedrin on false charges. In both cases innocent people were condemned to death because of the hatred of those who were offered the message of salvation.

St. Stephen's Gate, possibly the site of Stephen's martyrdom.

The Book of Acts provides other examples of the parallels between the deaths of Stephen and Jesus. A crowd of people brought by the Sanhedrin called for Jesus' crucifixion. Their demands were met by Pilate, who ordered Jesus crucified. The angry crowd surrounding Stephen rejected his testimony and took him out to be stoned. Many in the mob participated in stoning Stephen to death. Luke's account of Stephen's death also provides us with our first glimpse of Saul, who watched the proceedings approvingly. Saul would not know until much later how he would be brought to Christ as a result of Stephen's martyrdom.

The parallels between Jesus' and Stephen's trials and deaths should not surprise us. Jesus and Stephen appeared before a Sanhedrin composed of largely the same people. The Jewish leaders had successfully used false charges against Jesus and used the same tactic in dealing with Christ's followers. The Jewish leaders didn't realize that what they saw as their success was being used by God. God used the death of Christ to bring about the salvation of his people. And God used the death of Stephen to bring this salvation message to the world.

While people were stoning him, Stephen uttered two phrases that were similar to those Christ uttered on the cross. The first of Stephen's phrases was "Lord Jesus, receive my spirit" (Acts 7:59). This was quickly followed by "Lord, do not hold this sin against them" (Acts 7:60). The phrases that Jesus used, however, were spoken in reverse order. Looking at those gathered around him at the cross, Jesus said, "Father, forgive them, for they do not know what they are doing" (Luke 23:34). And just before his death, "Jesus called out with a loud voice, 'Father, into your hands I commit my spirit'" (Luke 23:46). Stephen's whole being was filled with the love and knowledge of Christ. Even in death he was able to remember the words that Christ had uttered as he brought about the salvation of his people.

Questions

1. What parallels are there between Christ's trial and death and that of Stephen?
2. What happened to the Christians in Jerusalem after Stephen's death?
3. Why do you think Luke mentions that Saul was present at Stephen's stoning?

5 On to Samaria

Acts 8:4–40

The Jews disliked their Samaritan neighbors, who occupied the geographical area adjacent to Judea. The Samaritans traced their ancestry to those Jews who were left behind at the time of the exile as well as the people who were sent to settle in the area by Israel's and Judah's conquerors. The Jews saw the Samaritans as inferior and rejected them. One of the reasons for Jewish animosity came from the fact that the Samaritans shared many religious beliefs with the Jews but also included those of other traditions. At the time of Acts, the Jews continued to hate the Samaritans because of their role in hampering the rebuilding efforts when the Jews returned from exile. By A.D. 300, the Jews had excommunicated the Samaritans.

Philip, like Stephen, was one of seven Hellenistic Jews chosen by the apostles to minister to the Christians in Jerusalem. After the stoning of Stephen, the Christians in Jerusalem were persecuted. As a result of the persecution, Christians left Jerusalem and brought the gospel message with them to their new homes. The persecution

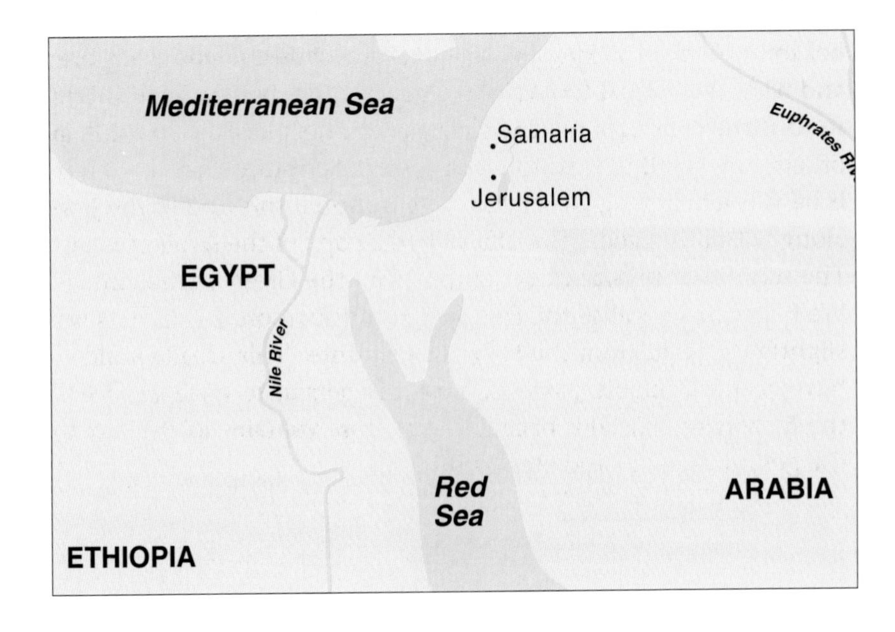

led Philip to leave Jerusalem and travel to Samaria. Scripture does not say whether Philip preached in the city of Samaria or in a city in the region of Samaria.

Philip's actions were not without precedent, because Jesus included the Samaritans in his public ministry. God blessed Philip's ministry, and many Samaritans came to believe in Jesus. When the church in Jerusalem heard of the Samaritans' faith, they sent the apostles Peter and John to the area. Peter and John witnessed the faith of the Samaritans and laid their hands upon the believers; the believers received the gift of the Holy Spirit. We do not know why the Holy Spirit did not come to dwell among the Samaritans immediately upon their acceptance of the gospel message. God may have withheld the gift of the Holy Spirit until the apostles arrived so that they could witness that salvation was for Jews and Samaritans alike. Later the apostles would understand that the gospel was to be brought to all people—Jews, Samaritans, and Gentiles.

At the height of Philip's work among the Samaritans, God called him to leave. Philip traveled south of Jerusalem to a road that led from Jerusalem to Gaza. Here Philip met an Ethiopian official whom God had prepared to hear the gospel message. Luke includes details about the Ethiopian that another writer might ignore. The Ethiopian had an important position in the court of Queen Candace. Candace was the title given to the queen mother of Ethiopia, who ruled on her son's behalf. The kings of Ethiopia were deified as young children and were considered too holy to carry out the daily tasks of ruling, so the king's mother ruled the country in his place. The Ethiopian official was familiar with the Jewish God. Scripture does not tell us if he was a believing Gentile or if he honored the God of the Jews along with other gods. The official had a copy of the scroll of Isaiah. The scroll that he was carrying was from the Greek Septuagint. We know this because the translation of Isaiah quoted in Acts was slightly different from the Hebrew Scriptures. This scroll would have been a valuable possession for any person to have, but for the Ethiopian official it become even more valuable as the way to the gospel message and eternal life.

Questions

1. What examples do you find in Scripture of how God blessed Philip's ministry among the Samaritans?
2. How did God prepare the Ethiopian for the gospel message?
3. What happened to Philip after he preached to the Ethiopian? (You may need to look beyond Acts 8.)

6 On the Road to Damascus

Acts 9

Saul was on the fast track to becoming a powerful member of the Jewish leadership in Jerusalem. Saul might have been a member of the Sanhedrin at the time of Stephen's stoning. If so, he would have had to be at least 30, because a member of the Sanhedrin had to be at the age of maturity. Saul had impeccable credentials for membership in the Sanhedrin. He had been born and reared in the city of Tarsus, which was located on the northwest corner of the Mediterranean Sea. The city was known for its medical school, clinic, and hospital. The educational system emphasized medicine as well as philosophy. Saul was reared as a strictly trained Jew in this educationally minded community. When Saul was twelve, his parents sent him to Jerusalem to study under the famous Jewish teacher Gamaliel.

The house of Ananias.

Not only was Saul well educated in the Jewish religion; he was also zealously committed to it. Saul saw the followers of Christ as heretics to the Jewish faith and way of life. He passionately persecuted the members of church and looked for ways of rooting out what he saw to be a false religion. Saul's determination led him to approach the Sanhedrin with a plan to capture Christians in Damascus and return them to Jerusalem for trial. The Sanhedrin primarily had jurisdiction over the Jews in and around Jerusalem, but its influence was felt in synagogues in other places.

Saul saw Damascus as an important location for stopping the spread of Christianity. Damascus was a Syrian city on the trade routes to the Roman Empire. If Christianity took hold in Damascus, it could quickly spread to the rest of the Roman Empire. Armed with this knowledge and a hatred of all things Christian, Saul headed to Damascus. The trip from Jerusalem to Damascus would have taken Saul between four and six days. This would have allowed him time to finalize his plans for imprisoning the Christians.

Saul appeared to have prepared for every possibility in his mission. What he did not count on was a dramatic encounter with the very person whose followers he was persecuting. Saul had heard the gospel message of Christ during his time in Jerusalem and had rejected it. God used a dramatic means of gaining Saul's attention and calling him to repentance and belief in Jesus. After Saul had seen a blinding light, Jesus called out to this most unlikely of followers, "Saul, Saul, why do you persecute me?" (Acts 9:4). Jesus' use of the word me indicated that by persecuting the church, Saul was also persecuting Christ. Jesus' call to Saul was clear and persuasive, and Saul believed.

Similarly Jesus calls to us in our sinfulness knowing that on our own we would never seek him. We don't know what God has prepared for our lives, but we must have a willingness to trust and follow him. Saul didn't know at the moment of his belief what God had in store for him. The same loyalty that Saul had shown to the Sanhedrin would now be directed toward Christ and his believers. If Saul had continued to persecute Christians, he may have become a powerful member of the Sanhedrin who achieved great success in his lifetime. But God had great things planned for him in spreading the gospel message and an eternal home with Jesus Christ, his Lord.

Questions

1. How had God been preparing Saul for his work as a missionary of Christ?
2. What did God tell Ananias that he had called Saul to do? How did Saul, later called Paul, fulfill his calling?
3. What joys did Saul immediately experience when he became a Christian? What were Saul's struggles?

7 Gathering the Gentiles

Acts 10–12

Peter remained in Joppa for a time after the miracle of raising Dorcas from the dead. While he was in Joppa, Peter stayed with Simon, a tanner. Simon's occupation as a tanner may at first appear to be extraneous information. However, as a tanner, Simon worked with the skins of dead animals, which made him ceremonially unclean under Jewish law. Peter would be considered unclean for staying in Simon's home.

Having contact with the skins of dead animals was not the only way a Jewish person could become ceremonially unclean. Jews would not enter the home of a Gentile because that too would make them unclean. After entering the homes of Gentiles, Jews would have have to take a series of lengthy steps to become ceremonially clean before they could worship God. This attitude toward Gentiles was deeply seated in the Jewish culture. From the time of Abraham, the Jews were God's covenant people. They had a special relationship with God that the other nations did not share.

Paul sailed past Crete on his way to Rome.

The Jewish people also followed strict dietary laws from the time of Moses. Animals were considered unclean if they did not chew the cud and had uncloven feet, if they crawled on their bellies, or if they died of natural causes (see Leviticus 11). An observant Jew would have been familiar with these restrictions. Eating unclean animals would be as repulsive to a Jew as entering the home of a Gentile or touching the skin of a dead animal. All of these contacts would have made the individual unclean and unable to worship God.

Timeline of Saul/Paul's Life

A.D. 5	Approximate date of Saul's birth
A.D. 35	Stephen martyred
A.D. 35	Saul's conversion
A.D. 38	Saul returns to Jerusalem
A.D. 43	Saul assists Barnabas in Antioch
A.D. 44	Herod Agrippa I dies
A.D. 46–48	First missionary journey
A.D. 50–52	Second missionary journey
A.D. 53–57	Third missionary journey
A.D. 57	Paul arrested in Jerusalem
A.D. 57–59	Paul imprisoned in Caesarea
A.D. 59–61	Paul imprisoned in Rome
A.D. 62	Paul released from Roman imprisonment
A.D. 62–67	Fourth missionary journey
A.D. 67–68	Second Roman imprisonment
A.D. 68	Approximate date of Paul's trial and death

When God called Peter to go the home of Cornelius in Caesarea, all of the laws about what was clean and unclean were called into question. Peter's relationship with Simon the tanner indicated that he was slowly moving away from Jewish law to Christ's law. God would use a repeated vision of clean and unclean animals to prepare Peter for Cornelius's request to come to Caesarea. Failing to follow dietary laws would be as incomprehensible to Peter as bringing the gospel to the Gentiles.

God made it clear to Peter, Cornelius, and all who were gathered in Caesarea that Christ's salvation had come for the Jews and the Gentiles. Peter hadn't even finished presenting the gospel when the Holy Spirit came on the people. The coming of the Holy Spirit to the Gentiles paralleled the outpouring of the Holy Spirit on Pentecost. "The circumcised believers [Jews] who had come with Peter were astonished that the gift of the Holy Spirit had been poured out even on the Gentiles. For they heard them speaking in tongues and praising God" (Acts 10:45–46). God's gift of the Holy

Spirit confirmed that the Gentiles were to join the company of those who believed in Christ.

Questions

1. Describe some of the ways that a Jew could become ceremonially unclean.
2. How did God prepare Peter to bring the message of salvation to the Gentiles?
3. How did the believers in Jerusalem react when they heard that Peter had baptized Gentiles? How did they react after hearing Peter's explanation (Acts 11)?

8 The Roman Empire Awaits

Acts 13–15:35

In looking back over the history of the early church, we cannot underestimate the significance of God's call to Peter to bring the gospel message to the Gentiles. Under guidance from the Holy Spirit, Peter presented the gospel to Cornelius, a God-fearing Gentile living in Caesarea. The outpouring of the Holy Spirit on Cornelius and those who believed with him showed that God wanted these Gentile believers to be in fellowship with him.

Acts does not record any immediate missionary journeys to the Gentiles following Peter's presentation of the gospel to Cornelius. Instead, most Gentiles came to believe in Christ incidentally. God-fearing Gentiles gathered with Jews at synagogues. When the apostles and other Christians preached in the synagogues, the God-fearing Gentiles heard the gospel message, and some became members of the early church.

God's call to Peter to minister to Cornelius was not a singular call to one individual. God wanted the early church to actively minister to Jews and Gentiles. The Holy Spirit called Saul, now referred to as Paul, and Barnabas to serve as missionaries. The church

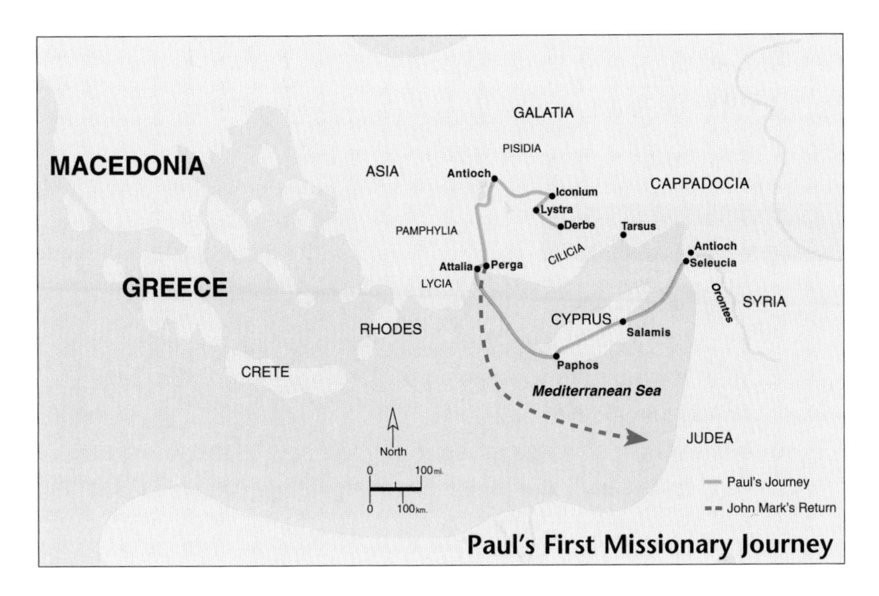

Paul's First Missionary Journey

in Antioch acknowledged the leading of the Holy Spirit and sent out Paul and Barnabas with prayers and encouragement.

The Gentile population was not the primary focus of Paul's and Barnabas's first missionary trip. Their ministry followed a pattern of first proclaiming the message of Jesus Christ at Jewish synagogues. When many Jews rejected the message of salvation, Paul and Barnabas brought the message to the Gentiles, many of whom accepted Christ.

The gathering of the Gentiles into the body of believers created some problems for the early church. Believers saw themselves as followers of Christ, but they were also tied to their Jewish roots and practices. Among the problems that the Christian church faced was whether the Gentile Christians were required to keep the Jewish laws. Jewish Christians who were former Pharisees wanted the new believers to observe the laws of Moses, just as they did. At first glance, this might seem to be a rather minor problem focusing on dietary laws. The underlying issue, however, had great significance for the church. Did a Gentile need to convert to Judaism before he or she could be a Christian? Because we have the benefit of history, our immediate answer is: of course not. Through debate and prayer the council of Jerusalem also saw that Judaism was not the door through which people had to pass in order to become Christians. God saved Gentiles as Gentiles and Jews as Jews. The Jerusalem council acknowledged that only through the grace of God did anyone come to salvation in Christ. Gentile believers were welcomed as equal members in Christ's church.

Questions

1. How did the church in Antioch support Paul and Barnabas before, during, and after their missionary trip?
2. What examples of the leading of the Holy Spirit do you find in Acts 13–15:35?
3. Some Jewish believers thought that the new Christians had to keep Jewish laws. Are there laws or traditions that we follow that keep others from becoming Christians?

9 Beyond Asia Minor

Acts 15:36—18:22

The good news of Jesus Christ spread quickly after his ascension. One of the reasons for this was the relative peace in the Roman Empire known as the *Pax Romana*. After a period of conquest and expansion, the Romans had settled into a time of building the infrastructure of their empire. Well-constructed roads allowed travel of up to 30 miles a day. Even leisurely travelers could journey about 15 miles a day.

Piracy on the sea had virtually been eliminated during the *Pax Romana*. Although sea travel was limited by the season, ships could sail up to 100 miles during a typical day. There were no passenger ships at the time; instead, passengers would board merchant ships to reach their destinations.

Paul and Silas traveled to cities in Asia Minor and then Europe to bring the message of Jesus Christ. Many of the places in which Paul preached had similar characteristics. As you learned in the last lesson, the cities generally had a synagogue where Paul would preach to Jews and God-fearing Gentiles. The cities were located at major crossroads. By preaching in these locations, Paul ensured that the

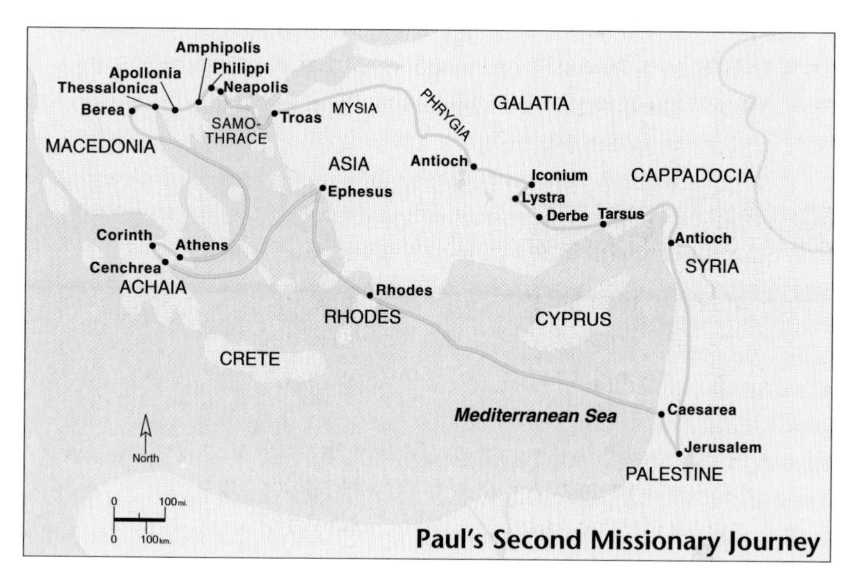

Paul's Second Missionary Journey

Stoics and Epicureans

The Book of Acts mentions two of the philosophies that Paul encountered in Athens. One was Stoicism, from which we get the word stoic. Stoicism arose from the teaching of the Greek philosopher Zeno (335–263 B.C.). He encouraged his followers to seek an absolute standard of good. Virtue would come through pursuing wisdom, serving others, and freeing oneself from passion. Peace of mind could be achieved through self-denial. Stoics encouraged political participation. They also taught that all people had access to the divine. Their idea of the divine was similar to pantheism in that god was present in everything.

The Temple of Zeus in Athens.

The second philosophical group that Paul met were the Epicureans, who followed the Greek philosopher Epicurus (341–270 B.C.). Unlike the Stoics, the Epicureans advocated withdrawal from public life. Their goal in life was to avoid pain. Ways in which this could be done included pursuing intellectual pleasures, striving for happiness, and living a contemplative life. While Epicureans acknowledged the Greek gods, they saw them as far removed from humans and their concerns. For some people, the Epicurean philosophy meant enjoying the finer things in life. Others equated the philosophy of Epicurus with hedonism.

good news would be spread to other cities and towns on those roads. Paul also preached at trading centers, where people from throughout the Roman Empire gathered for trade and commerce. The gospel message would be heard by these people and carried back to their cities and countries.

Paul was not alone on his second missionary journey. A disagreement between Paul and Barnabas about including John Mark caused the two men to part company. We aren't given the details of Paul's and Barnabas's argument, but we do know that many years later Paul and John Mark reconciled. While this disagreement might at first seem to be a negative, it enabled two groups of missionaries to go out and preach. Silas, a fellow believer from Antioch, accompanied Paul on this second journey. The two began their trip by encouraging the churches from Paul's first missionary journey.

In Lystra, Paul and Silas were joined by a young Christian named Timothy. It seems likely that Timothy became a Christian on Paul's first trip to Lystra. Timothy's father was Greek, and his mother was Jewish. He was probably in his teens when Paul first met him. Because his mother was Jewish, Timothy was considered Jewish as well, and he should have been circumcised at birth. The Jerusalem council indicated that God had accepted Gentiles as Gentiles into the body of believers. One of the ramifications of this decision was that Gentiles did not need to be circumcised when they became Christians. But when Paul planned to take Timothy along, he made sure that the young Christian became circumcised. The reason had nothing to do with Timothy's salvation. Paul knew that in order for Timothy to be effective in ministering to his fellow Jews, he would need to be circumcised as they were. Paul wanted to make sure that there would be no barriers in bringing the message of salvation to the Jews or Gentiles.

Questions

1. What were traveling conditions like during the *Pax Romana*?
2. How did the Holy Spirit lead Paul and Silas on their journey?
3. What criticism and persecution did Paul and Silas face as they preached the gospel?

10 Strengthening the Church

Acts 18:23—21:16

Paul did not have much time to spend in Ephesus on his second missionary journey. He promised the Ephesians that later he would return to them and preach the gospel of Christ. Paul kept his promise and remained with the Ephesians for about three years on his third missionary journey. By staying with them for an extended time, Paul could present the gospel and nurture the faith of the believers.

Like other cities to which Paul traveled, Ephesus was an important commercial and geographical center. Ephesus was one of the oldest settlements on the west coast of Asia Minor. It was a leading Roman city in the province of Asia, linking the western and eastern sides of the Roman Empire. The city's influence later declined as silt filled the harbor.

Ephesus was also the destination for many pilgrims. The temple to Artemis in Ephesus, one of the seven wonders of the ancient world, was four times as large as the famous Parthenon in Athens. The temple featured a sacred stone presumably sent down by the gods from heaven. Scholars now believe from the descriptions of

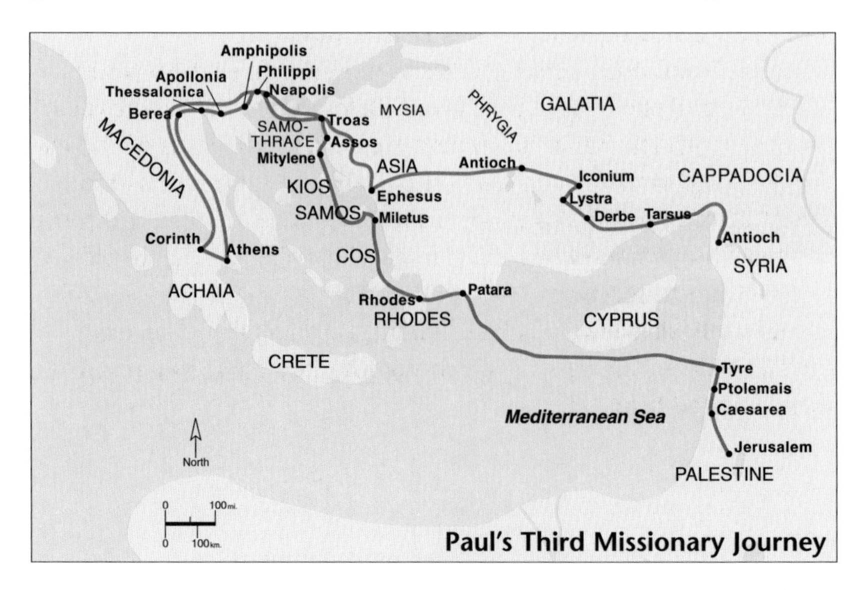

Paul's Third Missionary Journey

Ruins of the temple of Artemis in Ephesus.

this sacred stone that it was a meteorite. The temple was far more than a center of worship. Temple leaders also arranged loans for individuals and groups. A thriving souvenir business grew from the many visitors to the temple who wanted to take home an image of the goddess or her shrine.

Luke's account of Paul's time in Ephesus also mentions the Hall of Tyrannus. This building was most likely the school of a teacher of philosophy named Tyrannus. This school would have been in use during the morning, late afternoon, and evening. People would rest during the midday heat from 11a.m. to 4 p.m. Paul probably taught in the Hall of Tyrannus when it was not in use during these daytime hours. Since most of Ephesus took a break at this time, many people would come to hear Paul preach rather than rest. This schedule would also have enabled Paul to practice his trade of tentmaking and support himself in this way.

Paul left Ephesus thinking that he would never return to this great city and the believers he loved. Before traveling to Jerusalem, Paul met with the Ephesian leaders. He gave them words of encouragement and warning. He knew the trials and temptations that were particular to the Ephesians. Paul closed his remarks with words of Christ that were not recorded in the Gospels, "It is more blessed to give than to receive" (Acts 20:35). After a time of prayer, Paul left the Ephesian leaders for Jerusalem. Paul wanted to arrive in the city before Pentecost, even though he knew that certain hardships awaited him.

Questions

1. Why would Ephesus have been an important location for the spread of the gospel?
2. How did the information that you learned about Ephesus help you better understand the story? What information was extraneous?
3. Do you think that Paul should have continued his journey to Jerusalem or listened to those who warned him to stay away?

11 An Unlikely Path to Rome

Acts 21:17–26:32

The Jews from Asia had made spreading the gospel difficult as Paul traveled on his missionary journeys. Their efforts to keep Paul from spreading the gospel didn't end when he left their communities. They were determined to keep him from spreading the gospel anywhere and at any time.

When Paul arrived in Jerusalem, the Jews were looking for an excuse to end his work. The Christian Jews were aware of the animosity that Paul faced in Jerusalem. In an attempt to pacify their fellow Jews, they asked Paul to accompany four men who had taken Nazarite vows to the temple. Instead of avoiding trouble, Paul's visit brought him into direct conflict with the Asian Jews. They falsely accused Paul of bringing a Gentile into the temple. Gentiles were expressly forbidden from entering specific areas of the temple. The fact that Paul was innocent of these charges did not matter to the crowd, who wanted him killed.

The Romans were alerted to the riotous crowd and took Paul into custody, saving his life. Paul was brought before the Sanhedrin, the ruling religious leaders, to face charges. Following the death of Caiaphas, Ananias held the office of high priest. Ananias was known for his cruelty. A number of years later, a Jewish revolt broke out against Rome, and Ananias was assassinated by his own people. Paul used the dissension between the Pharisees and Sadducees in the Sanhedrin to his advantage. He stated that he believed in the resurrection of the dead, knowing that the Pharisees shared his belief and would side with him. The resulting argument in the Sanhedrin kept its members from making any decision about Paul.

Paul was taken here as a prisoner from Jerusalem.

Roman Citizenship

A person could gain Roman citizenship in a number of ways. The most obvious one was to be the child of a Roman citizen. Paul's Roman citizenship was a result of his father's citizenship. Roman soldiers could be offered citizenship when they retired from military service. Citizenship could also be given to a person as a reward for service to the empire or emperor. Finally, Roman citizenship could be bought. The punishment for those who claimed to be citizens but were not was death.

People who possessed Roman citizenship had rights and duties in the Roman Empire. Some of the rights were matters of convenience. For example, only Roman citizens could wear white togas. Roman citizens would also receive the best theater seats and places in line. People in the streets would make way for those they knew were Roman citizens.

Roman citizens were allowed to own property. They could vote and hold political office. A Roman citizen could not be punished unless a trial took place. Torture could not be used during questioning. Roman citizens also had the right to appeal their cases to Caesar. If at this point a citizen was found guilty, punishment could occur swiftly by the sword rather than the slow, agonizing death of crucifixion.

With Roman citizenship also came responsibility. Roman citizens were required to pay taxes, serve on juries, or testify in court when called upon. They would also be asked to serve in the army during time of war. People who became Roman citizens would be renamed. The first name would be a Roman name chosen by the individual and the second the name of the person's sponsor. The great Christian missionary Paul also had two names. Acts first referred to him as Saul, his Hebrew name; later he became known by his Roman name, Paul.

In order to protect his life, Paul was brought to Caesarea and appeared before the Roman governor Felix. The Jewish leaders sent a Roman lawyer, Tertullus, to present their case. Tertullus used flattering prose to address Felix but had no real charges to bring against Paul. In contrast Paul directly addressed Felix and explained his innocence. Rather than making a decision, Felix imprisoned Paul with the hope that Paul's friends would offer a bribe to have him released. Paul remained a captive of Felix until the governor was recalled to Rome because of irregularities in his rule.

Felix was replaced as governor by Festus. Festus was known to be a fair and just ruler but died after only two years in office. Paul was also called to defend himself before this Roman official. After languishing for a number of years without freedom, Paul asked to be tried before Caesar. In this way, Paul would finally be taken to Rome and achieve his objective of preaching to the citizens of this great city. Caesar and his representatives in Rome were the highest court of appeal. Festus had no recourse but to send Paul to Rome, where he would use the opportunity to spread the message of Christ.

Questions

1. Describe some of the people and groups that Paul faced as a result of his arrest.
2. How did Paul take advantage of various situations to speak about Christ?
3. What examples do you see of God being at work in the events of Paul's life in Jerusalem and later Caesarea?

12 A Roman Witness

Acts 27–28

The Book of Acts traces the movement of the church from being Jewish and in Jerusalem to embracing Gentiles and expanding to the capital of the Roman Empire, Rome. Acts opens with Jesus telling his followers to spread the gospel to all the world. Peter led the small band of Jerusalem believers in the first years after the outpouring of the Holy Spirit. As the church of Christ expanded throughout the world, Paul became the key figure in Book of Acts. His missionary journeys brought the saving knowledge of Jesus Christ from the Jewish center of Jerusalem to the Gentile center of Rome.

Paul's journey to Rome may not appear to have been a triumphant moment for the church. After all, Paul went to Rome not as a free man but as a Roman prisoner who had appealed his case before Caesar. But Paul did not let his circumstances dampen his enthusiasm for his mission of spreading the gospel to all those he encountered.

Because Paul was not a violent or typical criminal, he was allowed freedoms that most prisoners did not enjoy. At each port city, Paul visited with friends and encouraged the churches. He was

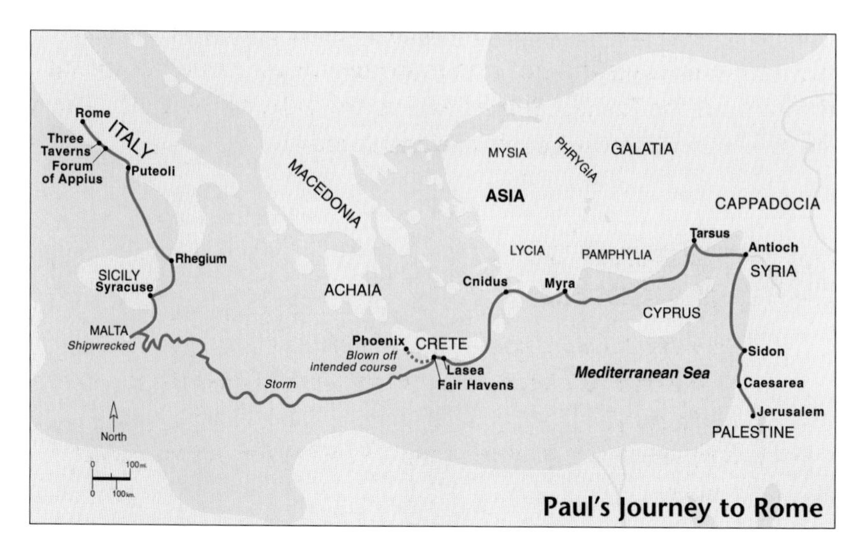

Paul's Journey to Rome

respected by the centurion Justus, who was charged with bringing Paul to Rome. The influence that Paul had on those traveling with him was probably best illustrated in his advice to the captain and crew during the storm. Although they had not listened to him when he told them not to set out from Fair Haven, they listened to him when they faced possible shipwreck. At Paul's urging, the crew ate a final meal on board the ship before throwing the rest of the food into the sea. Even in these tense moments, Paul paused with his shipmates for prayer. The next day, with the ship breaking apart, all 276 passengers arrived safely on the shores of Malta, just as Paul had said. Paul used his time in Malta to preach to the people there as well as his fellow travelers. Paul illustrated that even life-threatening circumstances provide opportunities for sharing the message of Jesus with others.

Even Paul's arrival in Rome did not appear to be that of a prisoner. Some believers from Rome traveled 30–45 miles to meet Paul, and they accompanied him to the city. In this city of about one million people, Paul would wait two years before his case would be presented before Caesar or one of his representatives. Paul's time was not wasted. He wrote the epistles to the Ephesians, Philippians, Colossians, and Philemon while he was under house arrest in Rome. Paul's guards allowed him visitors and opportunities to preach the gospel to those with whom he came in contact. What the Jerusalem Jews had tried to stop through false accusations and arrest worked only to bring the gospel message to a new, receptive audience. We know that the gospel message did not end in Rome but continued to spread throughout the Roman Empire and to the ends of the earth. The work of spreading the gospel continues today.

Questions

1. How did those on board the ship treat Paul?
2. How were Paul's imprisonment and trip to Rome used for God's glory?
3. Why was it important that Paul be able to present the gospel in Rome?

Writing to the Believers

1 Epistles: An Introduction

1 John 1–5

Paul and other church leaders did not abandon the churches they had planted after they left. Instead, they maintained contact with the churches through numerous letters. In the ancient world, letters were the most common way to communicate over vast distances. Letters would be carried by friends or strangers from one city to another. This method of delivering letters was unreliable, and few letters remain. The letters that survive from the first century do not all contain important information. Some letters contain orders that were to be carried out, and others contain information that we might consider trivial.

Paul walked into Rome along the Appian Way, one of the oldest Roman highways, which dates from 312 B.C.

The letters written by the apostles and other church leaders are often referred to as epistles. The word *epistle* indicates that these were not ordinary letters. The epistles to the early churches and believers were concerned with theology and morals. The Gospels were written after many of the letters, so the congregations could not read the Gospels to find the answers to their questions. Instead, they would write to Paul or another person to seek answers. Sometime later a letter would arrive answering their questions and encouraging them as they followed Christ. Some of the New Testament letters appear to be written so that they could be passed among churches. Generally the letters were written with specific people and situations in mind. One difficulty in reading the letters is that we do not have the questions that the letter answered. Some difficulties in interpretation could be easily solved if we knew the type of situation to which the author responded.

The epistles sent to the early churches and believers were generally intended to be read publicly. One of the reasons for this was that few people knew how to read. The letters were often addressed to congregations with the same questions and concerns, and in need of the same instruction. A public reading would ensure that all people knew how God wanted them to respond to the message of salvation. Even though the letters were written by Paul and others, we should not forget that they were inspired by God.

The public reading of the epistles assured that they would be heard in their entirety at one sitting. Similarly, we should read each epistle in its entirety at one time. One of the reasons for this is that each topic in the letter builds on the one before. Any argument or case that the author makes is built on earlier information in the letter. By reading only sections of the letter, it could be possible to take teachings out of context. When you are reading sections of an epistle in church or elsewhere, take the time to look at what comes before and after the section so that you have a sense of the major themes. Above all, read each epistle with the eagerness that you would read a letter from a friend you haven't seen in a long time. Even though these letters were written long ago, they are letters for you as well.

Questions

1. Why were letters such an important form of communication in the first-century world? How did people receive letters from others?
2. Why did the apostles and others write to the early churches and individual believers?
3. What are the different themes and ways in which the author presents love in 1 John?

2 Structuring the Letters

Romans 1:1–17; 16:25–27; 1 Corinthians 1:1–17; 16:5–24; 1 Peter 1:1–12; 5; Jude

The epistles were thoughtfully written letters to the early church and individual believers. The style in which the letters were written reflected the time period. The majority followed the customary format of a Greek letter with a salutation, body, and greetings. Some of the epistles followed the Jewish custom of including a section of thanksgiving. This section would appear after the salutation and reminded readers of God's goodness and the author's appreciation for the readers.

Ancient Corinth.

Paul used similar salutations in the letters that he wrote. Paul's greeting in 2 Corinthians is similar to those included elsewhere: "Paul, an apostle of Christ Jesus by the will of God, and Timothy our brother, To the church of God in Corinth, together with all the saints throughout Achaia: Grace and peace to you from God our Father and the Lord Jesus Christ" (2 Corinthians 1:1–2). Paul's greeting "grace and peace" combined salutations from Hebrew and Greek. "Grace" came from the Greek word *charis*, and "peace" came from the Hebrew word *shalom*. Even Paul's greetings reflected the fact that God had called Jews and Gentiles into his church.

The tone of most epistles is different from that in a letter we might receive from a friend. Personal comments play a minor role in the apostles' letters. The comments do show us that the letters were written to people who were cared for and known by the authors.

The apostolic letters were written as a teacher might address a student with questions about a topic. The questions that the churches asked have been lost, however, and we are left with only the replies.

It's also helpful to notice the literary features that the authors used when writing the letters. The authors used images and metaphors that would have been familiar to their audience. For example, Paul wrote to the Galatians, "Do not be deceived: God cannot be mocked. A man reaps what he sows. The one who sows to please his sinful nature, from that nature will reap destruction; the one who sows to please the Spirit, from the Spirit will reap eternal life. Let us not become weary in doing good, for at the proper time we will reap a harvest if we do not give up" (Galatians 6:7–9). Jesus also used metaphors about planting and harvesting in his preaching. For the Jews living in Palestine and the Gentiles in Galatia, the growing and harvesting of plants served as a metaphor to which they could relate. Paul's image remains relevant today as people continue to plant and harvest fields large and small.

As we analyze and dissect the letters, it's possible to lose sight of the fact that these are not ordinary letters in a literature book. These letters are the inspired Word of God. Yes, we see the authors' characteristics in the way that the letters were worded, but we also see God at work in addressing the church through the ages. Walter C. Kaiser explains, "The preparation that went into the lives, experiences, vocabularies, and outlook of the writers of Scripture was enormously significant. Thus, by the time they came to write Scripture, so authentic were the expressions that they used that any of us who might have known them prior to their writing of the text of Scripture would have instantaneously recognized that that is precisely how each writer spoke. The idioms, vocabularies, styles, and the like were uniquely their own, yet the product was precisely what God wanted as he stayed with each writer in such a way that there was a living assimilation of the truth—not a mechanical dictation of the words, such as a whispering in the writer's ear or an involuntary movement of their hands as they automatically wrote" (Walter C. Kaiser and Moisés Silva, *An Introduction to Biblical Hermeneutics* [Grand Rapids, Mich.: Zondervan, 1994] pages 181–82).

Questions

1. List three letters written by Paul that contain the greeting "grace and peace."
2. Why would the tone of the Epistles be different from one that we use when we write to friends?
3. You read about a metaphor that Paul used when he wrote to the Galatians. Locate two other extended metaphors used in the Epistles. Write down the metaphors and where they are found.

3 Words for the First Century and Today

1 Corinthians 5; 1 Timothy 5:1—6:2; Titus 2

While it's important to remember that the epistles were written for particular audiences, we need to be cautious not to leave these letters in the first century. As you have seen in the previous lessons, the world in which the authors lived played an important part in the way they wrote. Yet, as the inspired Word of God, the epistles were written to God's people for all times. Analyzing the letters in the context in which they were written and determining what applications they have for today's Christians present some difficulties. Gordon Fee and Douglas Stuart describe this dilemma: "The big issue among Christians committed to Scripture as God's Word has to do with the problems of cultural relativity, what is cultural and therefore belongs to the first century alone and what transcends culture and is thus a Word for all seasons" (Gordon D. Fee and Douglas Stuart, *How to Read the Bible for All Its Worth,* 2nd ed. [Grand Rapids, Mich.: Zondervan, 1993], pages 61–62).

Baptism of Christ **by Giovanni Agostino da Lode, 16th Century.**

Often we can use our common sense to determine whether or not a passage is relevant for us today. Specific commands presented to an individual about carrying out a task for the author probably don't apply to us. However, when we read in James 3 that we are to tame our tongues, we assume that these words remain applicable to Christians today.

We should also realize that a passage written in the first century cannot suddenly appear to be discussing twenty-first-century cultural items such as microwaves, televisions, or computers. That doesn't mean that Scripture doesn't give us general guidance regarding current technology. Again, as Fee and Stuart point out, "The problem here has to do with two kinds of texts in the Epistles: those that speak to first-century issues that for the most part are without any [contemporary] counterparts, and those texts that speak to problems that could possibly happen also [today] but are highly unlikely to do so. What does one do with such texts, and how do they address us? Or do they?" (*How to Read the Bible for All Its Worth,* page 67).

We need to find ways to bridge the gap from the first century to the twenty-first. Sometimes we may wonder how Christians can reach such different conclusions through their interpretations of the same Bible. For example, how can one group of believers conclude that infants should be baptized, while others believe baptism should take place by immersion when a person is older? Both groups understand that baptism is a necessary and important part of Christian life. In their arguments both groups acknowledge the importance of Jesus' baptism. But the biblical passages that the differing groups cite and the interpretation of these passages bring thoughtful Christians to different conclusions.

R. C. Sproul explains such difficulties this way: "What if after careful consideration of a biblical mandate, we remain uncertain as to the question of its character as principle or custom? If we must decide to treat it one way or the other but have no conclusive means to make the decision, what can we do? Here the biblical principle of humility can be helpful. The issue is simple—would it be better to treat a possible custom as a principle and be guilty of being over-scrupulous in our design to obey God; or would it be better to treat a possible principle as a custom and be guilty of being unscrupulous in demoting a transcendent requirement of God to the level of a mere human convention? I hope the answer is obvious" (quoted in Walter C. Kaiser and Moisés Silva, *An Introduction to Biblical Hermeneutics* [Grand Rapids, Mich.: Zondervan, 1994], pages 188–89).

Questions

1. What problems do Christians encounter when reading the Epistles?
2. Write down five themes or commands in the Bible that you think can be agreed upon by most Christians.
3. Read 1 Timothy 2. Write down three ways in which various parts of this passage could be interpreted.

4 Ephesians: The Church of the Triune God

Ephesians 1

Paul's letter to the Ephesians is generally dated to around A.D. 60. There is some question as to whether or not Paul wrote the letter. The opening verse that contains the words "Paul, an apostle" and "in Ephesus" does not appear in all early manuscripts. However, most scholars do accept Paul as the author of this letter and Ephesus as the church to which it was sent. At the time Paul wrote the letter, he was living in Rome under house arrest. During this time he also wrote Colossians, Philemon, and Philippians. All four letters emphasize the work of Jesus Christ to bring about the salvation of his people. Christ alone is the source of all Christian unity and joy. In his prison letters, Paul gave believers instructions about how they were to live out their faith in Christ in their daily lives and in the life of the church.

The Book of Ephesians is unlike Paul's other prison letters in that it does not appear to be written to a specific audience. Instead, Paul wrote a circular letter that would be read by the church in Ephesus along with surrounding congregations. Because Ephesians was not directed to a specific audience, the letter does not contain specific criticisms of false teachings or teachers who threatened the church. This enabled Paul to speak to more general matters of faith.

A statue of Artemis.

Paul's dominant image in the Book of Ephesians pictures the

church as a living organism. The church is the living body of Christ on earth. The temple of Artemis figured prominently in the Ephesian landscape and stood as a testament to the devotion of the believers in this goddess. Much of the Ephesian economy hinged on the money that pilgrims spent while visiting the temple. When Paul wrote the word *temple* to the Ephesians, his audience would not think of the Jewish temple in Jerusalem but the one to Artemis in Ephesus. Paul used the familiar image of a temple when telling the Ephesians that the church is not a man-made temple but a living one. The church's glory comes from its living members, and their lives serve as a testimony to their belief in Christ. Christ is the living head of the church in Ephesus and throughout the world.

The words *grace* and *peace,* which served as Paul's greeting to the church of Ephesus, are repeated throughout the letter. Paul wrote about God's gift of salvation to believers in Ephesians 2:8–9: "For it is by grace you have been saved, through faith—and this not from yourselves, it is the gift of God—not by works, so that no one can boast." Throughout the letter Paul emphasized how believers are redeemed through Christ's blood and should faithfully respond to that gift. One of the charges that Paul gave the church was to "make every effort to keep the unity of the Spirit through the bond of peace" (Ephesians 4:3). The words *grace* and *peace* that permeate the letter also serves as its conclusion: "Peace to the brothers, and love with faith from God the Father and the Lord Jesus Christ. Grace to all who love our Lord Jesus Christ with an undying love" (Ephesians 6:23–24).

Questions

1. When and where was the Book of Ephesians written?
2. What are some of the themes included in the letter to the Ephesians?
3. In the first chapter of the Book of Ephesians, Paul prayed. List two things that Paul prayed that the believers would receive from God.

5 Ephesians: The Church Body

Ephesians 2

Following his dramatic conversion, Paul dedicated his life to spreading the gospel message of Jesus Christ to the world. Paul used every opportunity available to him to tell others about Christ. Not even prison shackles kept him from sharing the message of salvation through Christ. When he was unable to be with churches personally, Paul wrote to them answering their questions and encouraging them in their faith.

Certain themes from Paul's ministry appear in many of the letters that he wrote. The universality of human sin is one of these themes. In a letter Paul wrote earlier to the Romans (3:23) he unequivocally stated, "all have sinned and fall short of the glory of God." Paul echoed these words in Ephesians 2:1, where he says, "you were dead in your transgressions and sins." Paul's gospel message began with humankind's need for a Savior. All people, Jew and Gentile, were unable to work out their salvation before God.

After Paul had established the need for a Savior, his letters centered on Christ's saving power as a gift from God. God sent Christ into the world to save his people from sin and certain death. Paul wrote to the Ephesians, "For it is by grace you have been saved, through faith—and this not from yourselves, it is the gift of God—not by works, so that no one can boast" (2:8–9). Paul wrote similar words to the Romans: "God demonstrates his own love for us in this: While we were still sinners, Christ died for us" (5:8). James Van Tholen explains the significance of Paul's use

A loose cornerstone (Ephesians 2:20).

of the word *yet* or *still* in Romans 5:6–8 this way, "The Greek word *eti* . . . means 'yet' or 'still,' and it makes all the difference between sin and grace. Paul writes that 'while we were still weak Christ died for the ungodly.' He wants us to marvel at the Christ of the gospel, who comes to us in our weakness and in our need. Making sure we get the point, Paul uses the word twice in verse 6 in repetitious and ungrammatical piling up of his meaning: 'Still while we were still weak, at the right time Christ died for the ungodly.'" (James Van Tholen, "Surprised by Death" *Christianity Today*, May 24, 1999, page 58.)

After explaining in his letters the need for salvation and the source of salvation, Paul went on to write about the joy of salvation. All who believe in Christ and receive salvation through him become members of "God's household" (Ephesians 2:19). You may remember from Paul's missionary journeys that when Lydia accepted the gospel message, so did all in her household. They were all baptized and became members of Christ's church. The term *household* would have been familiar to Paul's readers; a household included family members, staff, and even slaves. The household to which a person belonged would tell a great deal about that individual. To belong to God's household would have been the greatest honor imaginable. In his letter to the Galatians, Paul made the believers' place in God's household even clearer: "You are all sons of God through faith in Christ Jesus, for all of you who were baptized into Christ have clothed yourselves with Christ" (3:26–27). Not only are believers members of God's household; they are his sons and daughters!

Questions

1. How does Paul explain in his letters the need for salvation, the source of salvation, and the joy of salvation?
2. Find examples from two of Paul's letters explaining the need for salvation, the source of salvation, or the joy of salvation.
3. What does it mean to you that you are a child of God through Jesus Christ?

6 Ephesians: The Calling of the Church

Ephesians 3

Paul continued to build on his theme of the need for unity within the church body in his letter to the Ephesians. In Ephesians 2, Paul emphasized the oneness of Jews and Gentiles within the fellowship of believers. Ephesians 3 elaborates on Paul's theme of the members of the body of Christ being one. Paul explained to the Ephesians that Christians are to share a oneness with fellow believers just as they are one with Christ. All believers are members of one body—Christ.

Paul explained that the body of Christ is charged with carrying out Christ's work on earth. When an individual responds to Christ, he or she becomes a member of the body of Christ on earth—the church. Faith in Christ links believers to one another. Paul used the image of the family repeatedly through the Book of Ephesians. This image reminds believers that they are called to care for and love one another. Earlier in Ephesians Paul spoke of how believers came to belong to the household of God, in which differences are irrelevant and love envelops all.

Paul described the unity among believers as a *mystery*. Paul's use of the term mystery spoke of an insight or a truth that becomes available only through God's revelation to believers. The mystery that Paul presented was that Jews and Gentiles were united under Christ. You may remember that in the Old Testament the Jews were God's chosen people and were to be set apart from the Gentiles. Jews living in the Old Testament were not privy to the knowledge that one day Jews and Gentiles would be united in their faith. This unity would come only through the sacrifice of Jesus Christ. Paul emphasized this unity among believers in Ephesians 3:6, where he focused on the word *together*. "This mystery is that through the gospel the Gentiles are heirs together with Israel, members together of one body, and sharers together in the promise in Christ Jesus." Paul reminded the Ephesians that God had called him to bring the gospel to the Gentiles. Because of his missionary work with the Gentiles, Paul was now a prisoner of Rome.

Ephesians 3 concludes with Paul's prayer for the believers. Paul's prayer was not for new Christians but for those who were developing their faith. Paul prayed that the people would continue to grow in the knowledge of Christ. He also prayed that Christ's love would fill them. Paul indicated that God would continue to work in ways not completely understood by the believers. Just as the Old Testament believers did not grasp the unity of Jews and Gentiles that would be achieved under Christ, so the New Testament believers did not fully grasp God's power or purpose. Paul encouraged the believers to be rooted in the love of Christ so they could be filled with God's Spirit. Paul concluded his prayer by speaking of God's work in his church. "Now to him who is able to do immeasurably more than all we ask or imagine, according to his power that is at work within us, to him be glory in the church and in Christ Jesus throughout all generations, for ever and ever! Amen" (Ephesians 3:20–21).

Questions

1. What did Paul mean when he used the word *mystery*? What did he say the mystery was?
2. Why did Paul put so much importance on the church being unified?
3. What references did Paul make in Ephesians 3 to the three persons of the Trinity?

7 Ephesians: The Church in Action

Ephesians 4:1—5:20

Look under the word *church* in the yellow pages of any phone book and you may find headings similar to the following: Baptist, Baptist-Southern, Catholic, Missionary Alliance, Christian Reformed, Congregational, Episcopal, Greek Orthodox, Lutheran, and many others. The list of churches and denominations may make it appear that the church is more divided than united. Although the church on earth is not always unified, we can be confident that the church eternal will be.

In the letter to the Ephesians Paul spoke frequently about the unity of the church and how that unity is to be put into action. Paul reminded the believers that there is one body, Spirit, hope, Lord, faith, baptism, and God. As we look at Paul's list, it's interesting to note the way in which Paul paired the elements. The center of the list is the Lord. It's easy for us to understand that the Lord is to be the center of the church in order for unity and harmony to exist among the believers. Paul then expanded the list outward from the center. We see hope and faith linked, the Holy Spirit and baptism, and finally one body and God.

Two of the linked items serve as reminders of sacraments given by Christ. Jesus called his disciples to go out to the nations and baptize in the name of the Father, Son, and Holy Spirit. You may remember from your study of the Book of Acts that when believers

***The Last Supper* by Leonardo Da Vinci, 1495.**

came to Christ and were baptized, they were often filled with the Holy Spirit. Paul's list of being one in Christ connects the outpouring of the Holy Spirit and baptism. The second sacrament alluded to in the list is communion. On the night in which he was betrayed, Jesus held the Lord's Supper with his disciples. Jesus took bread and broke it to remind them that his body was broken for the sins of his people. Paul connects the body of Christ with that of his Father, who sent him to bring redemption to his people.

Faith and hope are also connected in Paul's list. Christians' hope and faith are ultimately tied to Christ. Without belief in Christ and his redeeming work, there is no hope for salvation. Paul encouraged the church to grow in faith and the knowledge of Christ. In his great mercy, God put in place ways in which the church could develop in faith and unity. Paul illustrated what this unity when he spoke of the church as being a body, a family, and a temple. Lawrence O. Richards elaborates on the illustrations when he writes, "Living in the body means each person ministers to other members, using the spiritual gifts supplied by God and developed by gifted leader. Living as members of the family means coming to know and care for one another deeply, expressing that care in openness, compassion, forgiveness, and a deep involvement in each others' lives . . . living together as a holy temple means rejecting dark things and building our commitment to goodness, righteousness, and truth. All of these are learned within the context of the new community, created and led by Christ" (Lawrence O. Richards, *The Teacher's Commentary* [Wheaton, Ill.: Chariot Victor Books, 1987], pages 927–28).

God has provided all that the church needs here on earth. God has equipped the church with a variety of people with many gifts and talents. It is the challenge of members of the church to work in harmony with one another so that God can be praised and the church of Christ can increase in wisdom and outreach.

Questions

1. How are baptism and the Holy Spirit tied together in the Book of Ephesians? How are communion and God united?
2. What are some of the specific God-given gifts and abilities that you see evident in your church?
3. What does it mean to you that the church of Christ is to be cooperative and not competitive?

8 Ephesians: Personal Relationships within the Church

Ephesians 5:21—6:9

Throughout the Book of Ephesians, Paul emphasized the importance of the church being united under Christ. The church of Christ is to be united as one body with Christ as its head. Paul followed his words about the unity of the church by explaining how the unified church is to behave. Paul concluded this section of his letter by stating that members of the church are to "submit to one another out of reverence for Christ" (Ephesians 5:21). Paul did not let this statement stand on its own but extensively explained the role that mutual submission plays in relationships within the church.

A Jewish bride.

At first the concept of submission may appear to be contrary to Paul's teachings on unity. Such a relationship implies that one person submits to the wants, needs, and desires of another person even if it is not what he or she wants. Paul did not leave his readers with this impression of submission from his examples. All the relationships that Paul described were modeled after those of Christ. One of the ways in which church unity can be achieved is in having members willing to submit themselves to one another and Christ. Only with mutual respect and obedience can the church operate in mutual love for one another and Christ.

The three relationships that Paul used to explain what he meant about the need for Christians to submit to one another include relationships in marriage, the family, and at work. In describing the marriage relationship, Paul also spoke of Christ's relationship with the church. Christ's great love for the church is like that of a husband for his wife. The type of love that a husband has for his wife should be like that of Christ, who willingly gave up his life for the church. Just as in all relationships, Christ's and the church's relationship has two sides. We know that while Christ can uphold his end of the relationship perfectly, the church cannot. Christ expects the church to willingly submit to him knowing that he will look for its best interests and needs. You may note that the pronoun *her* is used when speaking of the church. Paul described the role of the church as being like that of a wife to her husband. Paul conceded that the comparisons between the church and Christ and a wife and her husband are not adequate. Even if the couple were able to follow God's plan for marriage and "become one flesh" (Genesis 2:24), their union lacks perfection. The relationship between Christ and the church remains unfathomable. It cannot be explained in human terms. Paul described it as a "profound mystery" (Ephesians 5:32).

Paul's description of mutual submission did not involve labeling people as having either an inferior or a superior role. The members in all of the relationships have different roles to play and opportunities to show Christ's love. All positions in life—whether parent or child, teacher or student, coach or player, manager or employee —provide opportunities to serve God and others.

Questions

1. Why do you think that Paul chose to compare the relationship of Christ with the church to that of a husband and wife?
2. How do we show reverence to Christ in showing submission and obedience in our relationships with others?
3. What roles are a part of your life? How can you serve God and others in your various roles?

9 Ephesians: The Church in Conflict

Ephesians 6:10–24

Paul's letter to the Ephesians focused on God's desire for unity among Christians. Paul described this oneness under Christ by using images of a body, a temple, and a household. Paul's letter provided practical examples of how the unity among believers could be seen through submission to one another in the name of Christ. Paul acknowledged at the close of his book that the church would face challenges that would make following Christ and achieving unity difficult.

Paul encouraged the Ephesians to stand strong in God's mighty power. Paul used an extended military metaphor to describe how God has equipped the church to stand against Satan. God provides believers with weapons to defend themselves against "the powers of this dark world and against the spiritual forces of evil in the heavenly realms" (Ephesians 6:12). In times of persecution, the church may mistakenly focus on threats from earthly enemies. Paul explained that Christians face no ordinary enemy; instead, they do battle with Satan and his forces, who are members of the unseen world. Satan will do all within his power to break the unity of the church. He will work to divide a church so the unified images of a body, a household, and a temple will no longer apply. Christians are not to underestimate the devil and his powers.

Statue of a man in armor.

Paul told the Ephesians not to be discouraged. God will not abandon his people on the spiritual battlefield. God equips his people with the spiritual armor of faith. God provides believers with defensive weapons, some of which are the belt of truth, the breastplate of righteousness, and the shield of faith. These defensive weapons not only will protect individual believers but also when placed together will defend the church of God.

God provides his church with one offensive weapon—the sword of the Spirit. Paul described the sword of the Spirit as the Word of God. Christians are to be equipped with the knowledge of God's Word so that they cannot be manipulated by false teachings. God's Word can cut through the lies and falsehoods of others and provide words of truth in their place. During his earthly ministry, Jesus himself used God's Word to battle against Satan and his lies. When Jesus was tempted in the wilderness, Satan tried to use God's Word as a weapon. Satan misrepresented God's Word and passed it off as the truth. But Jesus knew God's Word and revealed Satan's false teachings. Jesus then used God's true Word to stand against the devil's temptations. Paul told the Ephesians that the only offensive weapon they needed to take into battle against Satan was God's Word.

Paul concluded this section of Ephesians by speaking of the need for communication between God's army and its leader. Believers need to communicate with God through prayer. Communication with God is essential in order to stand against the devil and his schemes. Believers are to pray for their needs as well as those of the church at large. Paul then asked the Ephesian church to pray for him. Paul knew the importance of prayer as he faced battle from seen and unseen enemies of Christ.

Questions

1. What offensive and defensive weapons are available in God's arsenal?
2. What challenges did Paul face as he wrote his letter to the Ephesians? How could he apply the armor of God to his situation?
3. What happens to a Christian with a chink in his or her armor?

Lifting the Veil

1 Ezekiel: An Introduction

Ezekiel 1–3

The Bible contains many different types of writing. In your study of the Old and New Testaments you have read poetry, prophecy, letters, and history. In this unit you will study apocalyptic literature from the Old and New Testaments. Biblical apocalyptic literature is also known as visionary literature.

Apocalyptic literature was not an unknown type of writing during Judah's exile or in the days of the early church. Other examples of apocalyptic literature survive from 200 B.C.–A.D. 200. Apocalyptic literature uses settings, events, and characters that are different from those in the everyday world. The world that listeners know is transformed into the unknown. Something from the ordinary world, such as time, can be reversed or slowed. Visionary literature does not always follow a linear pattern of time or story. Events may change from the present-day world of the author to a distant

Coast of the island of Patmos.

The New Testament Canon

The word canon originates from a Greek word meaning "reed." That word's meaning evolved to "bar," which indicates that something has been measured according to a specific standard. This definition is applied when we refer to the New Testament canon. That is, the books included in the Bible have met the standard that different people and groups had applied.

All of the books included in the New Testament canon were written in the first century A.D. At least nine different authors addressed the books to audiences within the Roman Empire. Most of the books were not circulated beyond their intended audience until the second century. None of the original manuscripts sent by the apostles remain. Some manuscripts may have been destroyed during times of persecution, while others were lost over time. The earliest fragments from the New Testament date to the second century A.D. The earliest surviving copies of the manuscripts are from the third century A.D.

Old balance scale.

The early church recognized the Old Testament canon as well as the words of Christ. Early church leaders quoted Christ and the Old Testament in their letters and Gospels. From the earliest days of the church, some first-century writings were considered to be the inspired Word of God while others were not. All the New Testament books considered God's inspired Word had Christ as their central theme. Most of the books selected to be included in the canon were written by the apostles. Among the apostles was Paul, whom Christ called on the Damascus road. Jesus had directed his apostles to preach and carry the gospel message to the ends of the earth. The apostles circulated Christ's message through the written and the spoken word.

Around A.D. 10, church leaders informally recognized some New Testament books. These books were largely drawn from those books that the early church leaders already used in teaching their congregations. The main criterion in determining the validity of a book was Paul's words in 2 Timothy 3:16–17, "All Scripture is God-breathed and is useful for teaching, rebuking, correcting and training in righteousness, so that the man of God may be thoroughly equipped for every good work." The early church leaders wrote lists of the letters that they deemed to be valid writings of Paul and other church leaders. Some of these lists were disputed by churches from different regions. References to New Testament books from early church fathers, such as Clement, also helped in determining which books should be included in the New Testament canon.

In the mid-300s to early 400, some regional church councils attempted to establish the New Testament canon. By the time these church councils met, much of the canon was informally in place. Until the Synod of Hippo in 393, Hebrews, Revelation, and some other books were questioned as to the appropriateness of their inclusion in the New Testament. The Synod of Carthage in A.D. 397 listed Old Testament and New Testament books to be included in the canon. The synod also encouraged reading the Holy Bible at worship, a practice that continues today. Periodically the church revisited the question of which books should be included in the canon, but the Testaments have remained virtually the same since the early days of the church.

time without warning. The use of visionary literature by a writer helps an audience to see things in a new and fresh way.

New Testament apocalyptic literature has its roots in the Old Testament books of Daniel, Ezekiel, and Zechariah, and parts of Isaiah. Apocalyptic literature usually was written during a time of persecution or oppression. Daniel and Ezekiel wrote during Judah's Babylonian exile. The apostle John wrote Revelation when he was in exile on the island of Patmos. John knew firsthand about the persecution that the fledgling church faced from the Romans and others. Daniel, Ezekiel, and John looked to a time when God would bring judgment on their oppressors and salvation to his people. In some cases the writers provided a specific time frame for God's judgments. In other passages God's judgment was sure, but the time in which it would occur was not.

The themes in apocalyptic literature are often presented as a vision or a dream. Hidden meanings and symbols permeate the language of the text. Numbers are also used symbolically by visionary writers. For example, the number seven represents completeness. Some of the symbolism that the writers use is obvious or understandable, but other symbols are unfamiliar to us. The original readers of the Old Testament and New Testament books of apocalyptic literature would have had a much better understanding of the visions and images than we do. The images that the authors used were familiar to their audiences. The meaning of some of the symbols has probably been lost or changed over time.

While Daniel, Ezekiel, and John provide us with visions of the truth, they do not provide us with the literal truth. The language and images of our world prove inadequate for the events that these writers describe. What is clear in all of the apocalyptic literature you will study is that God controls the seen and unseen world. At his appointed time, God will appear in triumph to judge all who oppose him and save those he calls his own.

Questions

1. List three characteristics of apocalyptic literature.
2. Why did John, Ezekiel, and Daniel write apocalyptic literature rather than letters?
3. Read Ezekiel 1:4–28. What are some of the images that Ezekiel described before he heard God's voice calling him?

2 Ezekiel: The Temple Destroyed

Ezekiel 8–11

The temple in Jerusalem served as the central worship site for God's people from the time of Solomon until their exile. Solomon's temple was not only a religious center but also a source of pride for the people of Israel. When the nation divided after Solomon's reign, Jeroboam set up alternate religious centers in an attempt to keep the faithful from traveling to Jerusalem. The Jerusalem temple was not the first structure that God's people used to worship him. At God's command Moses had directed the Israelites to build the tabernacle. The tabernacle traveled with the people throughout their desert wanderings and later became a permanent place of worship at Shiloh when the people settled in Canaan.

The Israelites were not unique in having a central place of worship. Other cultures in the Near East also had worship centers for their gods. You may remember that when the Philistines captured the ark of the covenant, it was placed in a temple erected to the god Dagon. The nations surrounding Israel viewed their gods as being confined to specific geographical locations. Because of these views about gods, it's understandable that some people in Israel and Judah shared a similar view of God. Some in Israel and Judah forgot the greatness of God and limited his power and might to their national borders.

Model of the temple.

The Israelites' belief that God dwelt within the Jerusalem temple was understandable. Their ancestors had seen God's presence come into the tabernacle in the desert and the Jerusalem temple. A year after being called by God, Ezekiel was given a vision that took him to the Jerusalem temple. Through this vision, God showed Ezekiel the depth of his people's sins, the coming destruction of the temple, and his presence extending beyond the temple or Jerusalem. Even in Babylonian exile God continued to be with his people.

One of the phrases repeated in Ezekiel's vision was "the glory of the Lord." In the Old Testament the phrase "the glory of the Lord" was often linked to God's revelation of himself. Ezekiel encountered God's glory on the plain in exile and in the temple. "And there before me was the glory of the God of Israel, as in the vision I had seen in the plain" (Ezekiel 8:4). As Ezekiel saw God's glory leave the temple, he knew the fate of Judah. The temple alone could not protect God's people if he was not present with them. Ezekiel understood that the Babylonians were unable to destroy the temple and Jerusalem on their own. By withdrawing his presence from the temple and Jerusalem, God allowed the Babylonians to destroy the temple and Jerusalem because of the sins of this people. The temple was destroyed not because God could not defend it but because he was no longer present with his people. The reason Ezekiel encountered God's glory in the plain of Babylon was because God's glory had departed from the temple and Jerusalem.

Questions

1. How did many people in Israel and Judah restrict God's power and presence?
2. Locate three places in Ezekiel 8–11 where the prophet used the phrase "the glory of the Lord."
3. How do people today restrict God's glory or presence?

3 Ezekiel: The Temple Renewed

Ezekiel 40:1–16; 43:1–12; 44; 47:1–12; 48:30–35

All three of Ezekiel's major visions were introduced with the phrase "in visions of God." The first vision was God's call to Ezekiel (Ezekiel 1). In Ezekiel's second vision, God showed him the destruction of the temple and Jerusalem. Ezekiel's final vision, which closes the book, took the prophet back to Jerusalem and the Temple Mount. In this final vision, God showed Ezekiel a new temple, which signaled God's return to dwell with his people. Ezekiel's vision was a prophecy of hope for God's people living in exile.

Ezekiel's vision of a new temple in Jerusalem blended events of the near and distant future. The temple in Jerusalem would be rebuilt when the exiles returned from Babylon. However, it would not be built on the grand scale of Ezekiel's vision or duplicate Solomon's glorious temple. The temple of Ezekiel's vision pointed to a glorious time when God would be present with his people. Ezekiel's vision would find fulfillment in Christ's coming, when he dwelt for a time with his people. The vision that God gave to Ezekiel also pointed to the time of Christ's second coming, when God will make all things new.

Ezekiel's vision was not the first time that God provided measurements to one of his servants concerning his temple. On Mt. Sinai God gave Moses blueprints for the tabernacle and its furnishings. Solomon's temple followed this pattern but on a larger scale. The pattern of the temple in Ezekiel's vision did not follow that of the Jerusalem temple, nor was it intended to serve as a blueprint for a later temple. The temple that Ezekiel described was symmetrical and built with great care. As Ezekiel traveled through the temple, he moved toward increasingly holy locations. Even in his vision Ezekiel did not enter the Most Holy Place, because only the high priest entered it once a year.

Finally, Ezekiel witnessed God's glory return to the temple. God's glory entered from the east entrance, which was where Ezekiel had earlier witnessed God leaving the temple. After God's glory returned, the east gate was shut. God's glory would never again leave the temple that Ezekiel viewed. God would dwell with his people forever. God's glory entering the temple summoned the people to renew their commitment to God. The temple was not a holy place because of the objects or the way in which it was built. Rather, the temple was holy because God is holy. Ronald E. Clements observed, "The temple was not simply a place in which worship could be performed; it was also a symbol of the spiritual meaning and godly foundation of the whole society." Ezekiel's vision of the temple and worship was far beyond what God's people could achieve on their own. In God's mercy, his people would return from exile and have the opportunity to worship him at a new temple in Jerusalem. Only in the new heavens and earth following Christ's return will they be able to perfectly fulfill the vision that God had given Ezekiel. Just as Moses had received a glimpse of the Promised Land, so Ezekiel was given a glimpse of a temple and people filled with God's glory.

Questions

1. Briefly describe Ezekiel's three major visions.
2. How did Ezekiel's vision mirror that of Moses?
3. How did Ezekiel's temple vision mingle the natural and supernatural worlds?

4 Daniel: An Introduction

Daniel 1:1–7; 2:24–49

Daniel's life spanned the time of Judah's exile. Daniel was between 15 and 18 years old when he was among the first group of exiles taken from Judah to Babylon. He was still living when some of the exiles returned to Israel. Daniel did not make the return trip, because he was elderly and the journey was difficult.

Daniel lived at a critical time in the life of God's people. God had fulfilled many of the promises that he had made to Abraham, Isaac, and Moses. The people of Israel had been a great nation and lived in the Promised Land. God had also fulfilled the warnings that he had given the people if they were disobedient. Because the nation failed to obey God, Israel never again rose to the position of prominence it had held under Solomon and David. In the years preceding the exile, God's people had become idolatrous. They had worshiped false gods and defiled the temple. After the exile, Israel was no longer identified as idolatrous. The exile had forced the people to turn from their idolatry and worship God alone. During the exile, God made new promises to his people. The coming Messiah and the return of the exiles to Israel were two promises that God directed the prophets to speak to his people.

Daniel by Michelangelo, c. 1536–1541.

Unlike Ezekiel, Daniel was not called by God to be a prophet. Daniel descended from an influential family in Judah, whereas Ezekiel came from a priestly family. Even though Daniel was not a prophet, God called him to an important task as an administrator within the Babylonian and Persian empires. God equipped Daniel with an excellent intellect and the ability to interpret dreams, and he sent Daniel visions.

The theme of the Book of Daniel is God's supreme reign over all of creation. The first half of the book focuses on God's control over kings and nations. The style of this part of the book is primarily historical. The second half of the book contains the visions that Daniel received from God. Daniel's visions portrayed a triumphant God who reigns supreme over the past, present, and future. Daniel's visions pointed to the near and distant future and a time when God and his people would emerge triumphant. These visions provided hope for Daniel and God's people as they lived in exile.

Many of Daniel's prophecies have come true. There is an uncanny accuracy about some events that took place before the time of Christ. Because of this, some commentators doubt the authenticity of Daniel's visions. These critics argue that someone else later wrote the visions in the Book of Daniel. This later date would permit an author to coordinate the visions with events. But accepting a different author and later date suggests that God lacked the ability to fulfill the visions he gave to Daniel. The later dating of the Book of Daniel also calls into question the theme of the book, which is God's control over all he had created. In the end, Daniel's visions should point us to God, who gave Daniel the visions, and who rules over the past, present, and future.

Questions

1. What is the theme of the Book of Daniel? How is this illustrated in the first and second halves of the book?
2. Why do some critics argue for Daniel being written at a later time?
3. Skim Daniel 1–7. How did God provide for Daniel and the people of Judah during their exile?

5 Daniel: Seventy Sevens

Daniel 9

Daniel was well versed in the words of the prophets. He knew the prophecies of Jeremiah and studied them while he was an exile. Jeremiah had warned the people of Judah of their coming exile if they did not turn from their evil ways. As Jeremiah preached these prophecies of doom, he also provided hope for the exiles. Jeremiah told the people of Judah, "But when the seventy years are fulfilled, I will punish the king of Babylon and his nation, the land of the Babylonians, for their guilt" (Jeremiah 25:12).

***Virgin Mary with Child,* artist unknown. The prophets spoke of the coming Messiah.**

Daniel knew that the people living in exile were approaching the end of the 70 years that Jeremiah had prophesied. Daniel also knew that God kept the words that he had spoken through his prophets. God's people were in exile, just as the prophets had warned, and Daniel believed that God would fulfill the prophecy of Jeremiah and return his people to Jerusalem. After studying the words of Jeremiah, Daniel pleaded with God to show mercy in returning his people to Jerusalem. Daniel acknowledged Israel's rebellion against God, his law, and his prophets. God had exercised his righteous judgment through the people's exile and the destruction of Jerusalem and the temple. Daniel knew that only through God's abundant mercy and grace could the people of Judah return to Jerusalem.

Immediately following Daniel's prayer, God sent him the angel Gabriel. Gabriel had a specific message for Daniel by way of a vision. Daniel's vision began with a decree of 70 sevens. These sevens may be interpreted as seven-year intervals of times. Some scholars have tried to calculate these sevens using varying mathematical formulas to determine when events of Daniel's vision occurred or would occur. By way of contrast, the sevens can also be symbolic, referring to God's perfect time or a completed period of time. This second reading provides greater flexibility in how scholars interpret Daniel's vision.

Most interpreters of the Book of Daniel agree that the 70 sevens are arranged into three time periods. The first period of seven sevens coincided with Judah's exile and return to Jerusalem. Daniel and the other exiles found comfort in this section of the vision. God heard the cries of Daniel and the others in exile and would return a remnant to Jerusalem.

The second period of 62 sevens followed the exiles' return to Jerusalem until Christ's coming. Many of the Old Testament prophets spoke of the coming Messiah, and Daniel's vision confirmed that the promised Messiah would come. God's words to the Old Testament prophets would be fulfilled at his appointed time.

The third period of time in Daniel's vision causes the most difficulty for scholars and lay readers. Even in the Hebrew, the language of this vision of Daniel is difficult to interpret. One interpretation of the final seven is that the events were fulfilled with the Messiah's coming and the destruction of the Jerusalem temple in A.D. 70. A second interpretation is that we are living in an interval before this final seven occurs and that the years immediately preceding Christ's second coming will coincide with the final seven. Scholars do not agree on a definitive interpretation of these verses from Daniel's vision.

The vision of the 70 sevens provided hope for those in exile. God had and would continue to fulfill the promises that he had made with his people. God had not forgotten them. The Messiah would come at God's appointed time. And one day God would dwell with his people forever.

Questions

1. What did Daniel conclude after studying the Book of Jeremiah?
2. What are some ways that the 70 sevens can be interpreted?
3. How would Daniel's vision provide encouragement for God's people living in exile?

6 Daniel: Israel's Future

Daniel 10–12

One of the reasons that some scholars have doubted the authenticity of the Book of Daniel is the vision described in Daniel 11:1–35. The details of Daniel's vision seem to be uncannily accurate. In reading other Old Testament prophecies, we see their fulfillment in more general terms. In Daniel's case minute details such as the marriage arrangements of future rulers were revealed and later fulfilled. In order to account for the accuracy of Daniel's vision, some critics have argued that the closing chapters of the Book of Daniel must have been written following the Maccabean revolt hundreds of years after Daniel's death. Others contend that the Book of Daniel was edited after the events in Daniel 11 occurred. This later editing added and changed details so that Daniel's words seemed remarkably accurate.

Persepolis, Xerxes' capital city.

Even before the birth of Christ, and up to the present, defenders of the Book of Daniel have pointed to the book's accuracy as God's special revelation to a man who remained faithful to God throughout the exile. The visions also are in keeping with the book's theme of God actively working in the lives of his people throughout time and history. At the close of the vision, Daniel admitted that he did not understand all that he had witnessed.

Daniel was probably in his 80s when God revealed this final vision. Daniel had spent at least 70 years in captivity. He was taken as a young man to Babylon, where he rose to prominence serving Babylonian kings. Later, Daniel achieved an important place in the Persian empire. Daniel did not accompany Zerubbabel and the others when they returned to Jerusalem. Reasons for this include that Daniel was elderly and that he may have been a key advisor to the king. Daniel knew he would not return to the land promised to his ancestors. Through a vision, however, God provided Daniel with a glimpse into what the future held for God's people, Israel.

The events recorded in the first 35 verses of Daniel 11 would prove to be accurate according to all historical accounts of the period. In Persia, a fourth king would appear who would be "far richer than all the others. When he has gained power by his wealth, he will stir up everyone against the kingdom of Greece" (Daniel 11:2). Daniel accurately described Xerxes I, who battled against Alexander the Great of Greece. Xerxes was unsuccessful in conquering the Greeks. As the Greek empire grew, the Persian empire declined.

Daniel's vision continued with a description of what would occur following Alexander's death: "his empire will be broken up and parceled out toward the four winds of heaven. It will not go to his descendants, nor will it have the power he exercised, because his empire will be uprooted and given to others" (Daniel 11:4–5).

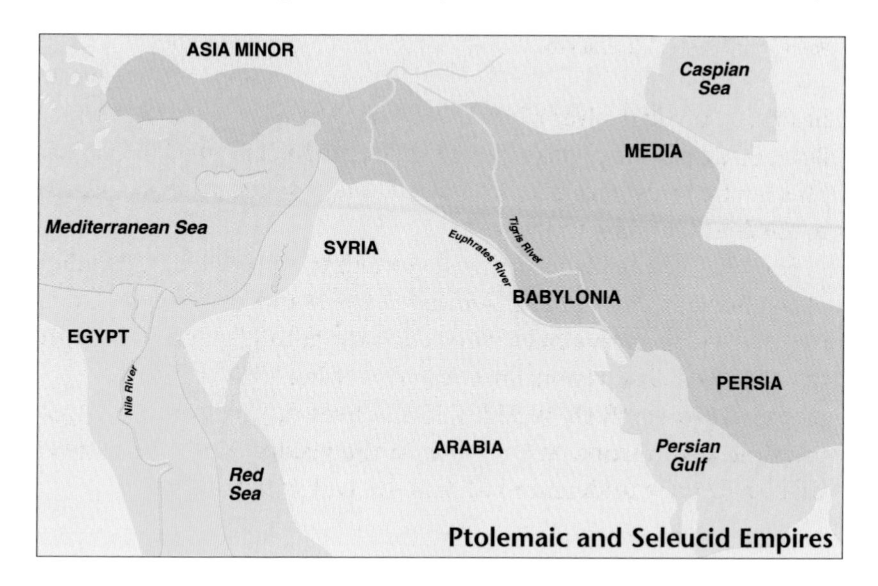

Ptolemaic and Seleucid Empires

Alexander's empire did not pass to his descendants. Instead, four generals divided the kingdom among themselves. Two of these generals were Ptolemy and Seleucus. Ptolemy and his descendants would rule the southern kingdoms, which included Egypt, while Seleucus and his progeny would rule the northern kingdoms, which included Syria.

The remaining verses of Daniel 11:1–35 describe the intrigue and fighting between and within the Ptolimies and Seleucids. Alliances between the empires to Israel's south and north would be made and broken; God's people were caught in between. Eventually Antiochus Epiphanes seized the Seleucid throne. Unfortunately, Daniel's vision of this ruler would prove accurate. Antiochus Epiphanes persecuted the Jews, slaughtering 80,000 of them, according to one account. He also sacked the Jerusalem temple and as a final insult dedicated it to Zeus. History shows that God did not abandon his people to the likes of Antiochus Epiphanes. A Jewish family, the Maccabees, as well as others revolted against the Seleucids. The temple in Jerusalem was reclaimed and the altar rededicated to the service of God.

Questions

1. How do different people account for the accuracy of Daniel's vision recorded in Daniel 11:1–35?
2. What had Daniel been doing immediately before he received this vision? How did his actions prepare him for what he was about to see?
3. List and explain three details in Daniel 11:1–35 that were fulfilled at the time of the Ptolemies and Seleucids. You may find a Bible commentary or a study Bible helpful.

7 Revelation: An Introduction

Revelation 1

The opening verses of the Book of Revelation identify John as the author of the book; however, they do not specify which John. Historically the apostle John has been considered the author of the Book of Revelation. The apostle John would have been elderly when he received the visions described in the final book of the New Testament.

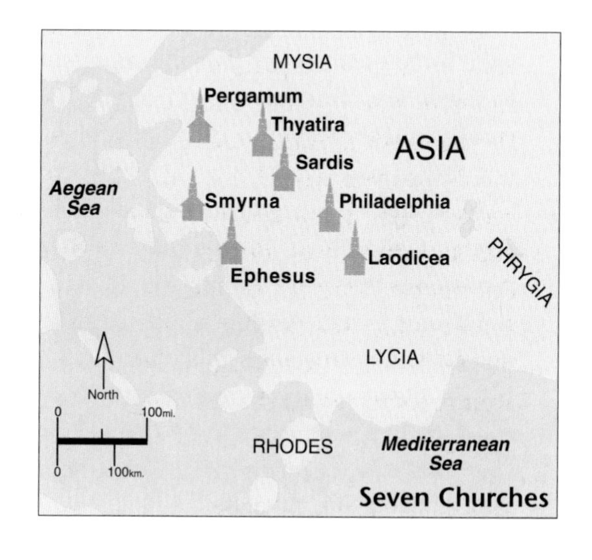

Seven Churches

John indicated that he was on the island of Patmos when he received a vision sent by God. Patmos was a rocky island located in the Aegean Sea southwest of Ephesus. The Romans used Patmos, as well as other islands, as a place to punish political prisoners. John stated that he was on the island because he preached the gospel of Jesus Christ.

John most likely wrote Revelation between A.D. 69 and 96, which roughly corresponded with the reign of the emperor Domitian (A.D. 81–96). Until the time of Domitian, the Romans considered the Christians a Jewish sect. The Romans permitted the Jews to practice their religion and exempted them from emperor worship. An investigation following the death of the emperor Nero determined that Christianity was not a Jewish sect but a separate religion. Christians did not receive the worship exemptions that the Jews did. Domitian insisted that people address him as "our lord and god." Christians refused to use this address and worship Domitian, so the church of Christ faced intense persecution under Domitian's rule. In this setting John wrote the words of the vision that he received from God.

Temple of Domitian in Ephesus.

John addressed his book to the seven churches of Asia Minor. You may recall that in the Bible the number seven is associated with completeness. These seven churches represented the church of Christ hearing Revelation. The churches were listed in the order that a courier would travel to deliver a letter to them. The churches were centrally located so that John's message would quickly travel to other churches in the region and throughout the empire.

In John's opening vision, he saw Christ standing among seven golden lampstands. John explained that the seven lampstands represented the seven churches to whom he was writing. It was significant for the original audience to know that Christ was standing among the lampstands, his churches. Christ was not absent from his people as they faced persecution. Even though the members of these churches could not see Christ in the flesh, they took comfort that Christ was among them spiritually.

Questions

1. What opposition did the church face when the Book of Revelation was written?
2. What was the significance of Christ standing in the middle of the lampstands?
3. In the opening eight verses, what does John indicate is the theme or purpose of the Book of Revelation?

8 Revelation: The Seven Churches

Revelation 2–3

While all books of the Bible are subject to a variety of interpretations, the Book of Revelation is even more so. Scholars have disagreed about how to interpret the symbols and images in the Book of Revelation. As you begin your study of Revelation, it is helpful to know about the major interpretations of the book. Some of these interpretations will not be relevant until later in your study of Revelation, but you will be better prepared if you are aware of differing views before you reach those passages.

The four main interpretations used in the study of the Book of Revelation are preterist, idealist, historicist, and futurist. The preterist view holds that the Book of Revelation contains no elements of prophecy or relevance for the future. The symbolism used in the book held meaning only for the people of John's time. All of the events described in Revelation were fulfilled during the days of the Roman Empire.

By contrast, a historicist reader understands that Revelation outlines the history of the church from Pentecost until Christ's second coming. The historicists hold to a more literal reading of the book than do people holding the other views. For example, the broken seals mentioned in Revelation are equated with the fall of the Roman Empire. The locusts that come from a bottomless pit are thought to refer to the Muslim invaders in European history. Not all historicists agree on the meanings of the symbols used in Revelation.

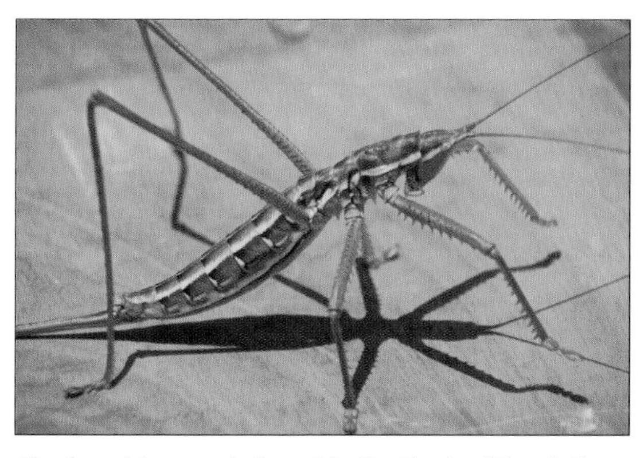

The locust is a symbol used in the Book of Revelation.

The futurists argue that Revelation 1–3 applies

to either John's time or seven eras of church history. Futurists say that from Revelation 4 to the end, events are described that will accompany the end times. There is some disagreement among futurists as to the rapture and how Christ will gather believers to himself upon his return.

The final major method of interpretation belongs to the idealists. For the idealist, Revelation is a picture of the epic struggle between good and evil. In this interpretation, symbols do not represent events in the past, present, or future. The Book of Revelation instead shows the triumph of Christ and his people over Satan and his followers.

Additional differences in interpretation come when we study the references to the millennium. Revelation 20 refers to a thousand-year reign of Christ, at which time Satan is bound. This thousand-year reign is known to Christians as the millennium. Even though the reference to the millennium does not occur until Revelation 20, it is beneficial to know the different viewpoints regarding the millennium as you read the chapters that precede it. There are three main views of the millennial reign of Christ, although there are other interpretations along with subgroups within these three views. The three primary interpretations of the millennium are known as premillenialism, postmillenialism, and amillenialism.

As you know, the prefix *pre* means "before". The premillenialists believe that Christ will return before the start of the millennium. Christ will personally reign along with his people for 1,000 years. Satan will then be unchained, and there will be a period of tribulation when those faithful to Christ are persecuted. After seven years of tribulation, Satan will be defeated and Christ's kingdom will be established. The premillenialist view is associated with futurists.

Historicists and preterists usually ascribe to a postmillenialist view. Looking at the prefix *post* is helpful in understanding the postmillenialist position. Postmillenialists believe that Jesus will come after 1,000 years of peace and prosperity. During this thousand-year period there will be a gradual conversion of people to Christ. Christianity will prove to be victorious in the world, and Christ will then return. Some proponents of postmillenialism expect a sudden rise in the evil in the world immediately before Christ's second coming.

Amillenialists form the final group for this discussion of millennial interpretations. Again understanding the prefix is helpful in understanding the views of this particular group. "Not" or "without" is the meaning of the prefix *a*. Amillenialists say that there will not be a literal thousand-year reign of Christ on earth. Christ's spiritual reign on earth began with his death and resurrection. The world will continue to be evil until Christ's second coming. At that time the dead will be resurrected and receive their eternal judgment. Christ will then establish and reign over a new heaven and new earth. People who follow an idealist reading of Revelation tend to follow the amillenialist view.

No matter how we interpret the Book of Revelation, we are assured throughout the book that God is in control over our world. He was with his people at the time the Book of Revelation was written, remains with his people today, and will be with his people in the future. The Book of Revelation assures us that Christ will come again and that those who are saved in his name will live with him forever.

Questions

1. What are the four primary ways of interpreting the Book of Revelation?
2. What are three views of Revelation's reference to the millennium?
3. How do preterists and futurists differ in their interpretations of the letters to the seven churches?

9 Revelation: The Seven Seals

Revelation 4–8:1

The opening verses of Revelation 4 move the reader with John from earth to heaven. John looked toward heaven and saw an open door. A voice that sounded like a trumpet invited him to see what lay behind the door. John's spirit entered God's throne room, and he stood face to face with God.

What John saw was beyond human description. John took what was most spectacular and beautiful in the world and compared these things with God's glory. Jewish tradition did not permit people to use God's name, and John did not use God's name either when he wrote, "There before me was a throne in heaven with someone sitting on it" (Revelation 4:2). John's subsequent description left no doubt that the someone he described was God.

Around God's throne John saw 24 elders. Scholars generally note that these 24 elders were the 12 patriarchs of the Old Testament and the 12 apostles of the New Testament. The 24 elders were dressed in white and had been given crowns of glory by God. Later John would see them lay down their crowns at the throne of God. The crowns that God had given the elders would be returned to him in worship.

John also saw four living creatures standing on each side of the throne. Bruce M. Metzger writes of these creatures, "John's description of the four living creatures on each side of the throne has a literary background that derives from the first chapter of the Book of Ezekiel. They represent the

John of Patmos, artist unknown.

cherubim, though John also supplies some of the features of the seraphim from Isaiah's vision of God in the temple. . . . The four creatures in John's vision have the appearance of a lion, an ox, a human being, and a flying eagle. These symbolize, respectively, what is the noblest, strongest, wisest, and swiftest in creation. In subsequent centuries it was customary to associate these four figures with the four evangelists, generally the man with Matthew, the lion with Mark, the ox with Luke, and the eagle with John. Such association, which is entirely fanciful, has influenced many forms of Christian art."

As John continued to peer into heaven, he saw Christ. Christ was introduced by using the messianic titles given in the Old Testament —the Lion of Judah, the Root of David, and the Lamb. John saw the Lamb of God looking as if he had been slain. The apostle John, generally considered the author of Revelation, had witnessed Jesus' crucifixion and understood what price Christ had paid for the sins of his people. John noticed that the same praise being given to Christ was given to God. Unceasing praise was brought before the throne of God.

Two chapters of praise precede the opening of the seals that brought God's judgment. The Old Testament repeatedly mentioned the holiness of God. God's people were to be holy because God is holy. As John looked into heaven's door, he witnessed a holy God who could no longer leave unpunished the sins of the world. The time for God's judgment had come. John's view of heaven provided hope for God's people in the midst of the images of God's judgment.

Questions

1. How did the different groups gathered around God's throne bring praise to God? What can we learn about praising God from these examples?
2. What references to the Old Testament do you see in Revelation 4–5?
3. How does John's vision of heaven provide comfort to Christians facing war, famine, or persecution?

10 Revelation: The Seven Trumpets

Revelation 8:2–11

John's vision of the seven angels with the seven trumpets immediately followed the opening of the seventh seal. John looked into God's throne room and saw seven angels standing before the throne. Many people throughout history have thought that Gabriel and Michael were among the seven angels, but there is no biblical basis for this belief. Each angel held a trumpet; the sounding of each trumpet announced the next series of judgments and events.

The organization of the series of visions involving the seven trumpet calls followed that of the seven seals. The visions involving the seals and trumpets began with a series of four closely related events. The first four trumpets brought God's judgment on humankind through creation. These judgments included God's wrath upon the land, sea, and inland waters and the sun, moon, and stars. Unlike the four horsemen of the apocalypse, who were given power over one-quarter of the world, the trumpet blasts signaled God's judgment upon one-third of the world.

***The Last Judgment,* by Michelangelo, c. 1536–1541.**

Following the first four judgments there is a brief intermission in John's vision. Similarly, between the fourth and fifth seal there is a pause. The fifth and sixth seals, along with the fifth and sixth trumpet blasts, are explained in rich detail. John wrote of plagues and devastation reminiscent of the Egyptian plagues. This time, however, God would bring about the final exodus of his people to their promised home with him. An interlude follows the sixth angel's trumpet call and that of the seventh. Just as with the seals, the seventh trumpet signals the next series of God's judgments.

John was presented with an additional visionary scene between the sixth and seventh trumpet blasts. John witnessed a mighty angel carrying a small scroll descend to the earth. One of his feet was on the land while the other stretched into the sea. John noticed that the scroll that the angel carried was different from what the Lamb of God had read. At the angel's instruction, John took the scroll and ate it. The scroll tasted to John like honey but soured his stomach. Ezekiel was also instructed to eat a scroll, which he described as tasting like honey in his mouth (Ezekiel 3:3). The word of God was sweet, even if what was written on it was bitter to those who would hear it.

John's vision continued as he viewed two witnesses testifying to God's word. God gave these two witnesses powers similar to those given to Moses and Elijah. They had the power to keep rain from falling and to bring plagues upon the land. Zechariah also spoke of two witnesses, Joshua and Zerubbabel, in his vision (Zechariah 3–4). Joshua represented the priestly office; Zerubbabel, the royal office. In the New Testament, Jesus sent out his disciples two by two to spread the gospel message. The two witnesses in Revelation prophesied for three and a half years, which corresponded with the first half of the final seven in Daniel's vision. After their period of prophecy the two witnesses were martyred. For three and a half days, the enemies of God rejoiced. Even death could not stop God's word, and in God's perfect timing the witnesses were returned to life. God's judgment would consume those who rejected him and his witnesses. The churches' mission to preach the gospel of Christ to all people had come to an end.

Questions

1. Compare the organization of John's visions of the seven seals and trumpets.
2. Write a lists of images and events from Zechariah 2–4 and those recorded in Revelation 10–11:14.
3. What is the role of the church in the time preceding Christ's second coming? How is this commented on in John's vision of the seven trumpets?

11 Revelation: Heaven and Earth

Revelation 12–14

One of the things that makes the Book of Revelation difficult is the unexpected switches in time. John seems to change at will from events in the past to those in the future. He also included events that seem to occur at the time of his writing. All of the time changes increase the difficulty in interpreting the Book of Revelation.

Revelation 12 seems to have taken place in the past. John told his readers that the great dragon he described was Satan. Whenever John stated what a symbol or image stood for, we must accept that as true and not insert our interpretations. John also described the child born to the woman by saying he would "rule all the nations with an iron scepter" (Revelation 12:5). This description makes clear that the child was Christ. John was not as clear about the identity of the woman. Some readers think that the woman was Jesus' mother, Mary. Others prefer a more general interpretation, such as that the woman represented the church of Christ.

The Dragon Wants to Devour the Infant, **by Giusto di Giovanni Menabuoi, 1363–1393**

Scholars do agree that there was a great battle between Satan and God. The great dragon did all within his power to destroy the promised child as soon as he was born. You may remember that King Herod attempted to kill Jesus. He ordered that all boys in Bethlehem aged two should be killed. God protected his Son by instructing Joseph in a dream to take Jesus and his mother to

Egypt. We know that Satan never stopped in his attempt to destroy God's plan for salvation.

John continued his account of the great dragon by telling of a battle in heaven between the dragon and his angels versus Michael and God's angels. The angel Michael was associated with God's people, Israel. Later Michael came to be associated with all of God's people, Jew and Gentile. We learn that in this cosmic battle Satan was defeated but had not yet met his final judgment.

Satan and his angels were hurled to earth, where Satan continued his pursuit of the woman. In this portion of the vision, John called to mind Old and New Testament events. Elijah hid from Ahab for about three and a half years before God called him to a dramatic encounter with the king on Mt. Carmel. Earlier in Revelation John mentioned a period of three and a half years when two witnesses would testify despite persecution. Following three and a half years, the woman was pursued again by the mighty dragon. This time God's creation kept her from harm. The earth opened up, swallowing the river that the dragon redirected in an attempt to drown her. This was not the first time that the earth is shown doing God's bidding. In Numbers 16 the story is recorded of the earth swallowing Korah, Dathan, and Abiram, who sinned by opposing Moses and Aaron.

The story of the great dragon is not finished. However, John never leaves any doubt that God will triumph. Satan may seem at times to have the upper hand on earth, but God's purposes will be done on earth as they are in heaven.

Questions

1. What do the dragon, the woman, and the child represent?
2. What examples of past, present, and future events are presented in Revelation 12–14?
3. What do we learn about God's character in Revelation 12–14? What examples of these attributes do we see in other parts of Scripture?

12 Revelation: The Seven Bowls

Revelation 15–16

The last of the series of seven judgments by God involved seven angels carrying seven bowls. The contents of the bowls were seven plagues that, when they were cast out, would complete God's wrath against those who had rejected him. This time God's judgments would not be limited to a quarter or a third of the earth. The whole earth would be affected by the outpouring of God's wrath.

John's vision of the angels carrying the bowls of God's wrath began in heaven with a vision of the faithful. John saw those who had stood against the beast gathered around a sea of glass mixed with fire. This sea serves as a reminder of the glassy sea before God's throne. The martyrs were given harps, which they used to praise God with a song similar to that of Moses. Just as Moses praised God for delivering the Israelites from the Egyptians, so the saints in heaven praised God for delivering them from those who had persecuted them. The martyrs lifted their song of praise thanking God for his mighty acts and just ways. The heavenly praise offered to God stood in contrast to the wicked, who refused to acknowledge God and faced his judgment.

A harpist.

The scene shifts from the faithful praising God to the angels who carried out God's judgment. The angels wore clothing made of linen and draped with a golden sash. The priests of Israel wore linen clothes as they led the people in worship. The golden sash would have been associated with royalty. The angels in the earlier judgments had carried out the role of prophets warning the people of the final judgments that were to come. The seven angels carrying out God's final judgments filled the roles of priests and kings.

Each of the seven angels in turn poured the contents of his bowl over the earth. Many of the plagues brought natural disasters in unnatural proportions. Yet God waited to pour out his final judgments until the last bowl was emptied. Every opportunity was given to those who had followed the beast to repent and turn to God. Rather than turn to God in their agony and repent, the wicked compounded their sin. John wrote that when the fifth plague was poured out on the throne of the beast, "Men gnawed their tongues in agony . . . because of their pains and their sores, but they refused to repent of what they had done" (Revelation 16:10–11). Even in the midst of unspeakable agony, the wicked refused to acknowledge their sins and repent.

The outpouring of the seventh plague completed God's judgment against those who refused to serve him as Lord and King. God's patience with the wicked ended. Repentance was no longer possible. A loud voice from the temple called out, "It is done!" (Revelation 16:17). Following the voice's pronouncement, lightning, thunder, a great earthquake, and hail from heaven descended upon earth and those remaining on it. All that the wicked had embraced had been destroyed. God's judgment had come from heaven. His wrath was completed. History had reached its end.

Questions

1. How did the angels carrying out God's judgment serve as prophets, priests, and kings?
2. Read Moses' song in Exodus 15:1–18 and compare this with the song in Revelation 15:3–4.
3. What opportunities during the last series of seven judgments did the wicked have to repent? How did they respond to these opportunities?

13 Revelation: Babylon, Beasts, and the Conqueror

Revelation 17–19

Five enemies of Christ are described in the Book of Revelation. The first is the great dragon, Satan. Other enemies include the beast of the sea, the beast of the land, the harlot of Babylon, and those wearing the mark of the beast. In the previous lesson you read of the defeat of those bearing the mark of the beast. Revelation 17–19 records the defeats of the harlot of Babylon, the beast of the land, and the beast of the sea. Satan's defeat follows in Revelation 20.

***The Beast Comes Out of the Sea,* by Giusto di Giovanni Menabuoi, 1363–1393.**

One of the seven angels with the seven bowls took John to see what happened to those God punished. John was transported to a desert. John did not see the virtuous woman who was earlier taken to the desert for protection from Satan and his minions. Instead, John saw a prostitute enjoying the company of the beast. John noted that the prostitute was richly robed but drunk with the blood of the saints. The woman's appearance masked her repulsive nature.

We know that the harlot symbolized Babylon, but we are not told what Babylon she represented. We know that the city of Babylon embraced all that the world saw as important. Babylon was a place of wealth, trade, and excesses.

John may have been referring to the city of Rome as the prostitute of Babylon. We know that Rome embraced the same types of excesses as did Babylon. During the Roman Empire, there were written accounts of wild orgies and persecutions of various groups and individuals for entertainment. By A.D. 100, half of Rome's population was made up of slaves. These exploited people, gathered from throughout the empire, were treated as commodities to be traded.

It's also possible the prostitute can be interpreted in a more general way. All people who pursue worldly vices can be described having the characteristics of the prostitute of Babylon. Even today people serve power, might, money, or national pride as a god. John warned of the destruction brought by the pursuit of earthly things. God's people are to serve him and him alone. A final interpretation to consider is that the city of Babylon will be revived one day and rise to prominence before Christ's second coming.

No matter what the interpretation of the prostitute of Babylon, John's description of what happened next is clear. An angel coming down from heaven announced, "Fallen! Fallen is Babylon the Great! She has become a home for demons and a haunt for every evil spirit, a haunt for every unclean and detestable bird" (Revelation 18:2). God's judgment had taken place. Babylon's destruction was no longer in the future but the past. All those who had aligned themselves with Satan were called to account. The beast of the sea, the beast of the land, the prostitute of Babylon, and those marked with the seal of the beast had been judged and destroyed. Only Satan's final demise remained.

Questions

1. Who are the enemies of Christ described in the Book of Revelation?
2. What are some of the interpretations as to the identity of the prostitute of Babylon?
3. What sins of Babylon do you see that are still embraced by the world?

14 Revelation: God's Holy City

Revelation 20–22

Christians throughout the centuries, as well as today, differ in their interpretations of the thousand-year reign of Christ described in Revelation 20:1–7. Despite these differing interpretations, we do know some things for certain. Christ will come again, and Satan and those with him will be defeated. Earlier in the Book of Revelation, John described the defeat of the beast of the sea, the beast of the land, the harlot of Babylon, and those identified with the mark of the beast. Finally the time for God's judgment has arrived. Satan and all with him received their eternal punishment. John wrote, "the devil . . . was thrown into the lake of burning sulfur, where the beast and the false prophet had been thrown. They will be tormented day and night for ever and ever" (Revelation 20:10).

***Christ Enthroned with the Apostles*, artist unknown.**

Satan's ultimate defeat did not conclude John's vision. Now John's attention turned to the throne of God and people from different walks of life standing before it. In his mercy, God delayed Christ's return so that people had every opportunity to turn from their wickedness and to God. John indicated that two different types of books were opened. The first book recorded the deeds of all the individuals standing before God's throne. We know that nothing found in this book would enable even one person to enter into eternal life with God. It was the second book, the Book of Life, that held the greatest significance for those standing before God's throne. Those whose names were written in the Book of Life had been saved by God through Christ's atoning work on the cross.

Between D-Day and V-Day

I lived through the dark time between D-Day and V-Day during World War II. In June 1944 the Allied forces landed on the beaches of Normandy, France. That was D-Day. At great cost, they knocked a hole in Hitler's "Atlantic Wall" and began their march to Berlin and the heart of Europe. We knew that the decisive battle had been won. On D-Day the outcome of the war was decided. Then there were days and weeks when we thought the war was just about over. We could not believe the Nazis might go on for more than a month. And yet the war lasted another eleven months. During those long, dark months, we who lived in Nazi-occupied territory suffered more than ever before. On May 5, 1945, we were free at last. That was V-Day, Victory Day.

When this world was invaded by the Son of God, when he died to remove the curse and rose to make a new beginning, we knew that the decisive battle had been won. And many thought and said that the war would be over soon, very soon. Christ's first coming was D-Day. Now V-Day is sure to come, but we don't know when. And just as we had to go through a dark, fearful and painful period before victory could be celebrated at the end of World War II, so Christians may have to go through many months of testing until, at last, all flags are flying, all tumult has ended and true shalom is here.

D-Day, Normandy, France.

Today it is not important that we know how long this period between D-Day and V-Day is going to last. Of the utmost importance is what we do while it lasts.

The Day of Christ's Return: What the Bible Teaches, What You Need to Know by Andrew Kuyvenhoven. Grand Rapids, Mich.: CRC Publications, 1999.

"If anyone's name was not found written in the book of life, he was thrown into the lake of fire" (Revelation 20:15). God's punishment on those who had rejected him was complete. Satan and all who followed him would spend an eternity together in the lake of fire.

John has nothing more to say about the devil and his followers. God's time of patiently waiting for them to turn from their sin and evil was over. The remaining chapters of Revelation turn to the wonder and beauty of God dwelling with his people forever. God's people were no longer scattered throughout the world among unbelievers. All his people were gathered before the throne of God in his holy city. Noticeably absent from the new Jerusalem, God's holy city, was the temple. The temple had been a centerpiece of Old Testament and New Testament life, but the temple was obsolete. John wrote, "I did not see a temple in the city, because the Lord God Almighty and the Lamb are its temple" (Revelation 21:22). All that the temple had symbolized for the Jewish people had been fulfilled. Christ had come and saved his people from their sins. He had returned again in glory. All who loved him had gone to live with him forever in a city with golden streets and eternal light. As Christians look at John's image of the new heaven and earth, we cannot help but repeat his refrain, "Amen. Come, Lord Jesus" (Revelation 22:20).

Questions

1. What is the significance of the two books that John described at the final judgment?
2. Why has Christ's return been delayed by many centuries?
3. Look at how the temple is described in 1 Kings 6. How does Revelation 21–22 illustrate that it is no longer relevant in the new heaven and earth?